READING
COMPREHENSION

ENGLISH
in context

Capitalization and Punctuation

Grammar and Usage

Reading Comprehension

Spelling

Vocabulary

Writing

Development and Production: Laurel Associates, Inc.
Cover Art: Elisa Ligon

SADDLEBACK PUBLISHING, INC.
Three Watson
Irvine, CA 92618-2767

E-Mail: info@sdlback.com
Website: www.sdlback.com

ISBN 1-56254-360-1

Printed in the United States of America
05 04 03 02   9 8 7 6 5 4 3 2 1

CONTENTS

● **Introduction** 5

UNIT 1 **Reading at Home** 6
LESSON
1 Unit Preview 6

● *Comprehension Skills Focus:*
Synonyms and Antonyms 7

2 Telephone Books 8

3 Medicine Labels 10

4 Pet Care 12

5 The Supermarket 14

6 Kitchen and Cooking 16

7 Home Entertainment 18

8 Laundry 20

● *Completing Analogies:*
Synonyms and Antonyms 22

● **Unit 1 Review** 23

UNIT 2 **Reading at School I** 24

9 Unit Preview 24

● *Comprehension Skills Focus:*
Classification 25

10 Science 26

11 Measures of Temperature 27

12 A Historical Document 28

13 Historical Timelines 30

14 Two Plans for Government 31

15 Latitude and Longitude 32

16 Using a Map 34

17 The Electoral College 36

18 Following Directions 38

● *Completing Analogies:*
Objects and Actions 40

● **Unit 2 Review** 41

UNIT 3 **Reading at School II** 42

19 Unit Preview 42

● *Comprehension Skills Focus:*
Sequence 43

20 Calendar 44

21 Detective Stories 46

22 Syllogisms 48

23 The Vocabulary of Literature 50

24 Famous Lines in Literature 52

25 Explorers of the New World 54

26 Inventions 56

● *Completing Analogies:*
Sequence and Degree 58

● **Unit 3 Review** 59

UNIT 4 Reading in the Community 60

27 Unit Preview 60

⬣ *Comprehension Skills Focus:*
Inference 61

28 City Maps 62

29 The Airport 64

30 Bus Route Map 66

31 The Mall 68

32 Voting Rights 70

33 Community Center 72

34 Driver's License 74

⬣ *Completing Analogies:*
Parts and Wholes 76

⬣ **Unit 4 Review** 77

UNIT 5 Reading in the Marketplace 78

35 Unit Preview 78

⬣ *Comprehension Skills Focus:*
Comparing and Contrasting 79

36 Housing 80

37 Credit Card Statement 82

38 Catalog Shopping 84

39 Catalog Order Form 86

40 Comparing Cars 87

41 Smart Shopping 88

⬣ *Completing Analogies:*
Cause and Effect 90

⬣ **Unit 5 Review** 91

UNIT 6 Reading in the Workplace 92

42 Unit Preview 92

⬣ *Comprehension Skills Focus:*
Word Analysis 93

43 Job Ads 94

44 The Employee Handbook 96

45 Memory Aids 98

46 Paycheck 100

47 Working Overtime 102

⬣ *Completing Analogies:*
Groups and Members 104

⬣ **Unit 6 Review** 105

⬣ **End-of-Book Test** 106

⬣ **Glossary of Terms** 110

INTRODUCTION

Think about this comparison: Is it difficult for you to bend, stretch, lift a heavy object, or run a few blocks if you need to? If so, many everyday activities in life will be difficult for you, too. Limited reading ability has much the same effect as limited physical ability. Is it hard for you to follow written instructions or directions? Do you have trouble figuring out unfamiliar words or remembering what you just read? These undeveloped skills, like undeveloped muscles, are life-limiting handicaps.

The lessons in this book can greatly improve your "reading fitness." Each lesson is an important skill-builder that can help you perform better at school, at work, and in the community. Why? *Reading* competence and *thinking* competence go hand in hand. Skillful readers are better at solving problems and making decisions. They finish their work faster and make fewer mistakes. They can detect clues in written information that help them stay focused on the main idea and "read between the lines."

Just as in body-building, *mental* skill-building takes practice. Your reading skills will get stronger every time you apply them to a real-life situation. If you're willing to work at it, you can become a stress-free reader who can approach any written material with confidence and ease.

READING AT HOME

FOR HELP WITH THE LESSONS, SEE THE GLOSSARY OF TERMS, PAGES 110–112.

UNIT 1

1 — UNIT PREVIEW

Where would you be likely to see each instruction?

A

Next to each instruction in the list, write a location from the box.
Then circle a letter to show the meaning of the instruction.

clothing care label	construction site sign	"no littering" sign
hand cream label	rental application	medicine label
game instructions	credit card statement	tomato can label

1. **Apply sparingly.** _____
   a. Wrap tightly.   b. Use a little bit.   c. Soak thoroughly.

2. **Remit in 30 days.** _____
   a. Wait for a month.   b. Answer immediately.   c. Pay in 30 days.

3. **Consult your physician.** _____
   a. Ask your doctor.   b. Tell about physics.   c. Get a physical.

4. **Violators may be prosecuted.** _____
   a. Violet rays may   b. Violence is not   c. Lawbreakers will
      harm you.   allowed.   be punished.

5. **Enter at your own risk.** _____
   a. Leave by the   b. Risk-takers need   c. Any consequences will
      rear exit.   not apply.   be your own fault.

B

Write a letter to match each important "warning word" with its *synonym*.

1. ____ **combustible**   3. ____ **perishable**   a. spoilable   c. burnable

2. ____ **prohibited**   4. ____ **hazardous**   b. dangerous   d. forbidden

C

Circle a word or words to correctly complete each sentence.

1. You can figure out how to operate an appliance by reading the
   (classified ads / owner's manual).

2. You need (assembly instructions / game rules) to put together a
   bookcase that comes in parts.

3. Understanding the terms of a product's (ingredients / warranty)
   can help you get a refund or a replacement.

USING SYNONYMS AND ANTONYMS

Words with the same or nearly the same meaning are called *synonyms.* **Words that have opposite meanings are called** *antonyms.* **Familiarity with synonyms and antonyms will make it easier to understand everything you read.**

A Write a *synonym* from the box for each **boldfaced** word. You will *not* use all the words in the box.

refrain	**denotes**	**ounces**	**remove**	**claim**
respond	**requires**	**portions**	**retain**	**revolves**

1. This bag of frozen peas contains four **servings** _____.

2. You must **reply** _____ to the landlord's letter within 24 hours.

3. That fabric won't **hold** _____ its color if you wash it in hot water.

4. The asterisk (*) next to that sentence **indicates** _____ an exception to the rule.

5. That little machine part **turns** _____ in a clockwise direction.

B Circle the *antonym* of each **boldfaced** word.

1. Her medical insurance is covered on a **group** policy.

    HMO   workers   individual   public

2. Thorough cleaning **retards** the growth of bacteria.

    limits   eliminates   prevents   encourages

3. Guests must park only in **designated** spaces.

    unmarked   designed   distant   disintegrated

4. You might **retain** water if you use too much salt.

    exclude   lack   reject   release

5. Carelessness can result in a **critical** injury.

    embarrassing   insulting   trivial   painful

2 — TELEPHONE BOOKS

The white pages of most telephone books begin with a listing of emergency numbers such as these.

FIRE: 911	POISON CONTROL: 555-1290
POLICE: 911	DRUG, ALCOHOL: 555-9812
HIGHWAY PATROL: 911	MISSING CHILD HOTLINE: 1-800-222-5678
AMBULANCE: 911	SUICIDE PREVENTION: 555-6666
COAST GUARD: 555-9182	FAMILY STRESS SERVICE: 555-4276
CHILD PROTECTIVE SERVICES: 555-3210	

A

Use information from the chart to complete the sentences or to answer the questions.

1. You see smoke coming from the window of an abandoned house. You should call _____.

2. Someone walking by your house falls to the ground and seems to be having a heart attack. Who would you call? _____ _____ At what number? _____

3. You witness a four-car collision on the freeway. You immediately use your cellular phone to contact the _____. What number do you call? _____

4. You overhear the unmistakable sounds of a neighbor beating his children. You call to speak to someone at _____.

5. A sudden storm is about to sink your fishing boat. You should notify the _____ at once. That number is _____.

6. Your uncle is depressed about your aunt's recent death. He tells you he's thinking of killing himself. What emergency service should help him? _____

7. Your baby sister appears to have been drinking paint thinner. You should call _____ at _____.

B

Yellow Pages headings are listed alphabetically by service. Read the example listings on the right. Use the information to answer the questions.

1. What two numbers could you call to compare charges for dog bathing?

   _____   _____

2. You want to buy a Siamese kitten. What store might be able to help you?

   _____

3. You have been dissatisfied with Pet Taxi's service. Who could you call to take your dog to the groomer?

   _____

4. You want to add some finches to your aviary. What store might have just the birds you're looking for?

   _____

   Where is the store located? _____

   _____ in _____

5. You want to put some water lilies in your aquarium. Where could you buy some?

   _____

6. What service offers both grooming and training for dogs?

   _____

   At what number? _____

7. You want to train your puppy to be a watchdog. What two numbers could you call?

   _____   _____

Pet Doctors

See Veterinarians

Pet Grooming

Bow-Wow Ltd.
   56 Bay Rd 349-6743
Canine Corps
   23 Hill Av 269-6704

Pet Shops

BIRD HAVEN

> Talking Parrots,
> Singing Canaries, &
> Other Birds
> 792-8134
> 27 Green Blvd.
> Midtown Mall

FIN TIME

> • Complete Line of
>   Tropical Fish
> • Aquariums
> • Water Plants
> 45 Lake Dr. 427-4156

Martin's Pets
   7 Salem St. 269-5673

Pet Training

Canine Corps
   23 Hill Ave. 269-6704

POLITE POOCH
   • Housebreaking
   • Chewing
   • Obedience
   • Protection
   792-4103
   52 North Street

Pet Transporting

PET TAXI

> "We Pick Up &
> Deliver Any Pet"
> 34 Main St. 792-6740

Will's Pet Transport
   2 James Pl. 591-5470

3 — MEDICINE LABELS

Understanding instructions on medicine labels can literally make the difference between life and death.

A

Study the medicine label. Then write a letter on the blanks to identify each part.

a. patient's name

b. physician's name

c. name of medicine

d. date prescription was filled

e. number of pills

f. throwaway date

g. prescription number

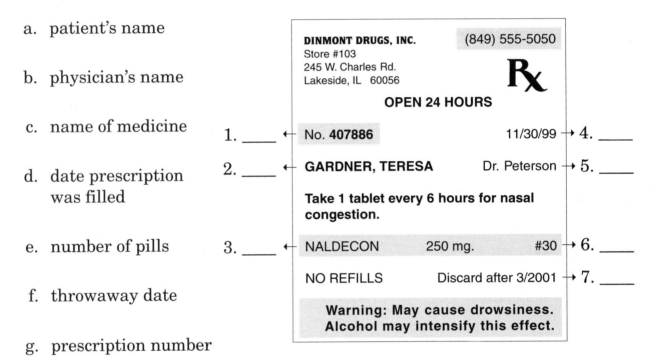

DINMONT DRUGS, INC.   (849) 555-5050
Store #103
245 W. Charles Rd.
Lakeside, IL 60056
Rx

OPEN 24 HOURS

1. ____ ← No. **407886**   11/30/99 → 4. ____

2. ____ ← **GARDNER, TERESA**   Dr. Peterson → 5. ____

Take 1 tablet every 6 hours for nasal congestion.

3. ____ ← NALDECON   250 mg.   #30 → 6. ____

NO REFILLS   Discard after 3/2001 → 7. ____

Warning: May cause drowsiness. Alcohol may intensify this effect.

B

Circle a letter to show how each sentence should be completed.

1. The maximum number of pills Teresa should take in 24 hours is

   a. 24.   b. 6.   c. 4.

2. By studying the label, you can infer that Teresa probably has

   a. a cold or an allergy.   b. sleeping sickness.   c. multiple fractures.

3. The dosage described as 250 mg must mean 250

   a. mammograms.   b. multigulps.   c. milligrams.

4. If Teresa takes three pills a day, this medicine will last for

   a. 30 days.   b. 10 days.   c. two weeks.

5. If Teresa drinks beer while she's on this medication, she may

   a. become an alcoholic.
   b. be too sleepy to drive safely.
   c. have violent stomach cramps.

6. After March 2001, the medicine prescribed for Teresa will

   a. no longer be effective.
   b. mysteriously disappear.
   c. turn into aspirin.

C

Over-the-counter medicine is often taken to reduce a fever or to relieve minor aches and pains. Study the label below. Then circle a word to correctly complete each sentence.

1. Children should take (fewer / more) tablets than adults.

2. The amount of acetaminophen in each tablet is (50 / 500) milligrams.

3. A child under the age of six (should / should not) take this medicine.

4. An acetaminophen tablet (does / does not) contain aspirin.

5. A 13-year-old should take the (adult's / children's) dose of acetaminophen.

STAYWELL Pharmaceuticals
A<u>===</u>**EXTRA STRENGTH** **CETAMINOPHEN**
Non-Aspirin Pain Reliever
100 **TABLETS**—acetaminophen 500 mg. each **SAFETY SEALED**
DIRECTIONS: **Adults:** 2 tablets every 6 hours **Children 6 to 12 years old:** 1 tablet every 6 hours **Children under age 6:** Consult a doctor. **WARNING:** If you are taking other medication, consult your physician before using this product. If symptoms persist for more than 10 days, see a physician. Keep the bottle cap tightly closed.

6. A doctor's approval is recommended for people who (are / are not) taking other medications.

7. A "safety sealed" product is protected against (tampering / misuse).

8. The two words used interchangeably on this label are (persist and consult / physician and doctor).

4 — **PET CARE**

Responsible pet owners are always looking for better ways to care for their animals. Your pet might thank you for studying the information in this lesson!

A

Study the pet care chart.

	CATS	DOGS	FISH
HANDLING	Lift a cat using two hands, one under its forelegs and one under its rump. A cat should not be dropped, for it will not always land on its feet. Brush its coat regularly.	Don't allow a dog to roam freely. Groom a dog regularly. Check that its ears are clean and its nails are trimmed. To avoid the loss of its natural oils, bathe it only when it is dirty.	Don't mix large and small fish. Net fish gently. To prevent the spread of diseases, isolate each new fish for a few days before adding it to your tank.
FEEDING	Bones that may splinter should not be fed to cats. Provide a high-protein, high-fat, commercial cat food. If food is not moist, provide water.	Serve a balanced diet of commercial dog food. Feed once or twice a day, depending on the dog's condition. Give the dog large uncooked beef bones or artificial bones. Provide water.	Check with the fish dealer about the proper diet for the fish. Don't put more food in the tank than the fish can eat in 5 minutes. After 10 or 15 minutes, all leftover food should be removed to prevent an accumulation of rotting food.
HOUSING	A box with a cushion or a blanket can be used for sleeping. Provide a scratching post to keep claws worn down.	Protect the dog from dampness and from extremes of heat and cold. A warm, dry blanket can be used for bedding. Clean the bedding regularly.	Don't use fish bowls because the fish can't get enough oxygen. Use distilled water. Provide proper lighting. Be sure the water does not contain chlorine.

Now use the information from the pet care chart to help you decide whether each statement is *true* or *false*. Write *T* or *F* on the blank.

1. _____ The healthiest dogs are bathed every day.

2. _____ Cats should not be fed chicken bones.

3. _____ A fish eats all it needs within five minutes.

4. _____ Dogs with heavy coats need no protection from cold weather.

5. _____ All kinds of fish can live together happily.

6. _____ Always use two hands to pick up a cat.

B

Circle a letter to show how each sentence should be completed. Use the *boldfaced* words as clues. if you need help, look back at the pet care chart.

1. **Commercial** pet food is

   a. made at home.　　b. sold in stores.　　c. poor in quality.

2. If a dog's skin loses its **natural oils**, it will become

   a. dry and scaly.　　b. soft and moist.　　c. red and patchy.

3. When you **isolate** a new fish, you

   a. put its bowl in the closet.　　b. introduce it to your other fish.　　c. keep it away from your other fish.

4. If leftover food **accumulates** in a fish tank, it will

   a. make your fish very fat.　　b. rot and cause disease.　　c. be eaten later as a midnight snack.

5. Tropical fish won't get enough **oxygen** if they

   a. are kept in a bowl rather than a tank.　　b. don't breathe deeply.　　c. lack a well-balanced diet.

6. A basic **grooming** tool for both dogs and cats is a

   a. stethoscope.　　b. bucket.　　c. brush.

C

Read about three popular pets. Use words from the box to complete the sentences. You will *not* use all the words.

tropical	learned	breeds	names	comfortable
ancestry	furry	pets	purebred	inborn

There are many (1) _____ of cats. Two major types are short-hair and long-hair. The bird-chasing activity in cats appears to be (2) _____.

A mongrel is a dog of mixed (3) _____. A (4) _____ dog has parents whose lineage has been unmixed since the breed was recognized.

More fish are bought than any other (5) _____.

(6) _____ fish don't feed in the dark. Water temperature must be between 70° and 80° F.

How familiar are you with "grocery store language"?

A

Study the supermarket ad.

FRANKLIN'S FINE FOODS

Fourth of July Spectacular!

We've got everything you need for your holiday picnic. Stock up early while supplies last. These terrific prices effective June 30 through July 6.

BONELESS BARBECUE STEAK **$1.99** lb. Cut from the cross rib. Just marinate and grill. (SAVINGS OF $1.50 PER LB.)	***FRESHEST CUT-UP FRYERS*** **.75** lb. Everyone loves barbecued chicken. Delivered to our store within 24 hours of processing! (SAVINGS OF .74 PER LB.)
SUPER-SWEET WHITE CORN **5** for **$1** All large, full, hand-picked ears! Certified to contain no detected pesticide residues. (SAVINGS OF 80 CENTS)	***LOCALLY GROWN MAMMOTH STRAWBERRIES*** Beautiful, sweet, and juicy! The finest grown anywhere. **$1.49** 16-oz. container (SAVINGS OF 55 CENTS)

Use information from the ad to answer the questions.

1. What is the regular price of boneless barbecue steak? _____

2. If you buy three pounds of chicken on sale, what is your total savings? _____

3. Suppose you need 2½ pounds of strawberries to make ice cream. How many containers will you buy? _____

4. Eight people are coming to your Fourth of July picnic. If five ears of corn are $1, how much does one ear cost? _____ How much for eight ears? _____

5. What word describes the process of soaking food in a flavored liquid before cooking it? _____

B

Read the phrases from the supermarket ad. Circle a letter to show the meaning of each phrase.

1. **Stock up early while supplies last** suggests that you

    a. buy stock in the company while business is booming.

    b. hurry to buy the sale items before they're all gone.

2. **Prices effective June 30 through July 6** suggests that

    a. prices will be lower on June 29 and July 7.

    b. prices will be higher before and after the sale date.

3. **Certified to contain no detected pesticide residues** is

    a. an official guarantee that no traceable insect poison remains on the product.

    b. a warning that all pesticide leftovers must be registered with the U.S. Post Office.

C

Here are some good tips for food shoppers. Circle the words that correctly complete the sentences.

1. Nationally advertised brands cost (more / less) than store brands or generic brands.

2. Meat, milk, and cereals are three of the four food groups necessary for a balanced diet. The fourth food group is (fruits and vegetables / snacks and treats).

3. Labels on cans and jars of food list information about (the nutritional value of ingredients / which stores have the best prices).

4. Food labels (do / do not) show the number of calories in each portion.

 •••••••••••••••••• **JUST FOR FUN** •••••••••••••••••••

Fact or fantasy?

1. Draw a star if spaghetti sauce contains maple syrup.

2. Draw a happy face if 3/4 cup is more than 2/3 cup.

3. Draw a triangle if *slice* and *dice* are synonyms.

6 — KITCHEN AND COOKING

How well do you know your way around the kitchen? Read the recipe for *gazpacho*. Have you ever tried this delicious cold soup?

GAZPACHO (serves four)

1 medium-sized cucumber, finely chopped
½ cup chopped onion
2 large tomatoes, finely chopped
½ cup green bell pepper, finely chopped

2 cloves garlic, minced
½ habanero chile, stemmed, seeded, and minced
3 cups tomato juice
1 tablespoon red wine vinegar

A

First, make a shopping list of the ingredients you will need to make gazpacho. Write your list on the lines.

_____   _____

_____   _____

_____   _____

_____   _____

B

What steps would you take to prepare this dish? Number the steps in order.

_____ Peel, chop, or mince vegetables.

_____ Serve icy cold.

_____ Purchase ingredients at the grocery store.

_____ Cover and refrigerate until chilled.

_____ Stir ingredients until thoroughly blended.

_____ Combine all ingredients in a glass or plastic bowl.

C

Draw a line to match each word on the left with its definition on the right. Use a dictionary if you need help.

1. **stemmed and seeded**   a. chopped into very tiny pieces

2. **minced**   b. a section of a garlic bulb

3. **clove**   c. removed from the vegetable

4. **chopped**   d. cut into small pieces

D

Are you familiar with the names of basic cooking utensils?
Unscramble the words to name each utensil pictured.

1. **CRITCLEE RINGFY NAP**

   _____

2. **DONWOE OPSON**

   _____

3. **EBRAGTEEG**

   _____

4. **RUNIGMASE SNOOPS**

   _____

5. **SERTOPDOHL**

   _____

6. **LEECRICT REXIM**

   _____

7. **LATEM ATPAULS**

   _____

8. **BERRUB PASLAUT**

   _____

9. **GINXIM LOWBS**

   _____

10. **SEAMGRUIN SCUP**

    _____

11. **ICEOOK ETHES**

    _____

E

Use the unscrambled words to answer the questions.

1. Which utensil would you use to turn pancakes? _____

2. Which non-electric utensil has a moving part? _____

3. Which two items run on electric power? _____

   _____

4. Which item protects the cook from harm? _____

7 — HOME ENTERTAINMENT

Do you watch much TV? What's *your* favorite form of home entertainment?

Read the prime time TV schedule for Monday night.

MONDAY EVENING						
	8:00	**8:30**	**9:00**	**9:30**	**10:00**	**10:30**
2	Buddies	Travel Magazine	NFL Football: Washington at San Diego			
3	Wonders of Nature		Mystery Movie: Dark Secrets			
5	Medical Miracles	Hollywood Hotline	Circus Special			News
9	Buddies	Hobart Hospital	NFL Football: Washington at San Diego			
10	Strike It Rich	Music U.S.A.	Night Hawk		D.C. Lawyers	
11	Celebrity Interview		ABC Movie: Cattle Drive			
13	Strike It Rich	Music U.S.A.	Night Hawk		D.C. Lawyers	
28	Classic Comedies	Live from the Met: Madame Butterfly				
63	Great Museums	Dinner with Chef Chu	The Congo: A Documentary		Masterpiece Theater	

Use information in the schedule to answer the questions.

1. How many hours are covered by this schedule? _____

2. How many channels are listed? _____

3. Which channels are showing *Strike It Rich*? _____

4. Which program lasts 90 minutes? _____

5. Suppose you don't get home from your baby-sitting job until 8:30. Will you be able to watch *Buddies*? _____

6. Does the schedule tell you whether *Masterpiece Theater* is airing a new program or a rerun? _____

7. If you don't like football, what movies could you watch while the game is on? _____

8. You are writing a report about Renaissance art. What program might help you with your report? _____

9. Your grandfather is an opera lover. What program is he likely to watch? _____

10. Which program would give you the latest gossip on your favorite film stars? _____

B

Does your family enjoy playing games? Think about how a game of *Bingo!* is played. Number the steps in order from 1 to 9.

_____ If the numbers are correct, the player wins. But if the Caller finds an error on the player's card, the player forfeits all five numbers and play continues.

_____ The Caller shouts out the letter and number on the ball.

_____ Players cover the free space with a marker.

_____ If two players claim a win at the same time—and both are found to be correct—each may shake a ball from the dispenser. The higher number wins.

_____ Play continues until a player shouts "Bingo!" to signal that he or she has covered a complete row of five numbers.

_____ The Caller distributes cards and markers to players.

_____ If they have that number on their cards, players cover it with a marker.

_____ Play stops until the Caller verifies the win by having the player read back the numbers that are covered.

_____ The Caller shakes a numbered ball from the dispenser.

LAUNDRY

Do you know how to keep your clothes looking clean and fresh?

Read the instructions on the left and the bleach label on the right.

SORT BEFORE LAUNDERING

1. Separate light colors from bright or dark colors. Man-made fibers will pick up color if washed with garments that are not colorfast.

2. Separate fabrics that require hot water and vigorous washing from fabrics that require cold water or short wash times to prevent fading.

3. Avoid washing "lint givers" with "lint receivers." Some items that release lint are chenilles, towels, and rugs. Some items that attract lint are corduroy, permanent press clothes, and any fabrics with man-made fibers.

 CITRUS FRESH BLEACH

Use to bleach white and colorfast fabrics only. Test to be sure before bleaching articles made of acrylic, nylon, polyester, and rayon.

BLEACH TEST: Mix 1 tablespoon of bleach with 1 quart of water in a glass, rubber, porcelain, or plastic container. Soak a small piece of fabric in a place that doesn't show.

WARNING: If bleach splashes on skin or in eyes, flood with water and call physician. If swallowed, give milk and call physician.

Now write a letter to match each term on the left with its definition on the right. Reread the labels above for help.

1. _____ **fabric**

2. _____ **washing action**

3. _____ **colorfast**

4. _____ **natural fibers**

5. _____ **lint**

6. _____ **man-made fibers**

a. tiny bits of thread and fluff

b. synthetic; made from chemicals

c. organic, made from living matter

d. churning movement

e. non-transferable dyes

f. material woven from fibers

Circle a letter to correctly complete each sentence.

1. Two examples of *man-made* fibers are

   a. silk and wool.   b. polyester and rayon.   c. straw and hay.

2. Two examples of *natural* fibers are

   a. cotton and linen.   b. nylon and velour.   c. grease and oil.

3. Shirt fabric that is 50% cotton and 50% polyester would probably

   a. transfer color.   b. shed lint.   c. attract lint.

4. The recommended water temperature for washing wool is

    a. not mentioned in the instructions.   b. very hot.   c. between 100° and 140° F.

5. A fabric that has a permanent press finish

    a. can't be bleached.   b. never needs ironing.   c. should be dry-cleaned.

6. In order to conduct a bleach test, you need a quart of water and a

    a. cup of bleach.   b. teaspoon of bleach.   c. tablespoon of bleach.

7. The warning on the bleach label indicates that bleach can

    a. irritate your skin and eyes.   b. be mixed in a metal bowl.   c. be swallowed with milk.

C

The warning on the right appears in the operator's manual that came with the washing machine. Use the information in the warning to help you decide how to complete each sentence. Circle the correct word.

1. A substance that can quickly turn into a dangerous gas is called (gasoline / volatile).

2. Putting a gas-soaked rag in the dryer could cause (a mechanical breakdown / an explosion).

3. To *comply* with a warning means to (compose / obey) it.

4. An item with a volatile substance on it should first be handwashed with a (detergent / stiff brush).

5. Two examples of volatile substances are (sparks and lightning / gasoline and kerosene).

> ### CAUTION
>
> Never put highly volatile substances like gasoline or kerosene into a washer or dryer. Washable articles with highly volatile substances on them should never be put in a washer or dryer. FAILURE TO COMPLY WITH THIS WARNING COULD RESULT IN A FIRE, EXPLOSION, OR SERIOUS BODILY INJURY.
>
> All items with volatile substances on them should be HAND washed with a detergent until no trace of volatile substance remains. The articles can then be machine washed. Only after thorough handwashing and machine washing should the article be placed in the dryer.

SYNONYMS AND ANTONYMS

Word analogies state the relationships between words and ideas. Many standardized tests require you to complete analogies. The analogies on this page will develop your understanding of *synonyms* (words with the same meaning) and *antonyms* (words with opposite meanings).

EXAMPLES: synonyms: *Healthful* is to *nutritious* as *toxic* is to *poisonous*.
Small is to *tiny* as *big* is to *large*.

antonyms: *Hot* is to *cold* as *black* is to *white*.
Fake is to *genuine* as *counterfeit* is to *authentic*.

◆ Follow the directions. Try not to use a word more than once.

acquire	stagnant	insufficient	terminate	purchase
review	following	malignant	disguise	exhibit
hasten	display	preceding	violent	savage
allow	prohibit	crafty	tender	gentle
shrewd	dismal	bleak	auspicious	heartening

1. Choose two *synonyms* from words in the box. Write them on the lines.

   _____   _____

2. Choose two *antonyms* from words in the box. Write them on the lines.

   _____   _____

3. Complete each analogy with a word from the box.

   a. *Dawdle* is to *loiter* as *hustle* is to _____.

   b. *Active* is to *passive* as *dynamic* is to _____.

   c. *Kind* is to *benign* as *cruel* is to _____.

   d. *Recall* is to *remember* as *recollect* is to _____.

   e. *Begin* is to *initiate* as *end* is to _____.

   f. *Something* is to *nothing* as *abundant* is to _____.

4. Choose four words from the box to write an analogy relating *synonyms* (as in the first set of examples). Write your analogy on the line.

   _____

5. Choose four words from the box to write an analogy relating *antonyms* (as in the second set of examples). Write your analogy on the line.

   _____

A Circle a word to correctly complete each sentence.

1. Look in the (white / yellow) pages of the telephone book for listings of stores, products, and services.

2. (Prescription / Over-the-counter) medicine must be ordered by a doctor.

3. After 15 minutes, you should remove any food that your (cat / fish) has not eaten.

4. Food labels list information about the (inspirational / nutritional) value of the food's ingredients.

5. Instructions for both recipes and games should be followed (in sequence / at random).

6. A TV schedule can tell you (how and why / when and where) a program will be broadcast.

7. Two well-known (organic / synthetic) fabrics are nylon and rayon.

8. *Defy* is to *disobey* as *obey* is to (*comply* / *reply*).

B Use the clues to help you complete the crossword puzzle.

ACROSS

1. Two natural fibers in fabrics are cotton and _____.

2. Add _____ to your wash to whiten clothes.

4. Sale prices are in effect for only a _____ time.

6. _____ name products are more costly than generic products.

8. _____ pet food is sold in stores.

DOWN

1. The instructions on a medicine _____ are extremely important.

3. Call 911 if you need _____ service.

5. Use a metal _____ to turn over pancakes.

7. A _____ of medicine is the amount you take at one time.

READING AT SCHOOL I

FOR HELP WITH THE LESSONS, SEE THE GLOSSARY OF TERMS, PAGES 110–112.

UNIT 2

9 — UNIT PREVIEW

It is your first day at a new school. How will you find your way around?

Study the map to answer the questions. Circle a letter to complete the sentence or answer the question.

NINTH STREET

| FRONT STREET | | | | | | CLARK STREET |

ROOM 1 | ROOM 2 | ROOM 3 | ROOM 4 | CAFETERIA

OFFICE | | | LUNCH TABLES | GYM

AUDITORIUM | ROOM 5 | ROOM 6 | ROOM 7 | SCIENCE LAB

10TH STREET

1. Your bus drops you off at the corner of Clark and 10th streets. You are closest to the
   a. science lab.
   b. auditorium.
   c. gym.

2. To get to the school office, you must go
   a. west. b. east. c. south.

3. The office faces
   a. Clark Street.
   b. Front Street.
   c. Ninth Street.

4. The school secretary gives you this map and tells you to see Miss Mack in room 4. You leave the office and walk
   a. east. b. west. c. south.

5. Room 4 is on which side of the campus?
   a. south b. north c. east

6. As you're buying lunch, you notice that the cafeteria is directly across from
   a. the science lab.
   b. room 1.
   c. the auditorium.

7. To get to your PE class in the gym, you go
   a. north. b. west. c. east.

8. At the end of the day you return to 10th and Clark to catch your bus. What corner of the campus is this?
   a. the northwestern corner
   b. the southwestern corner
   c. the southeastern corner

CLASSIFICATION

Grouping ideas or things into appropriate categories is called *classification*. This is an important thinking skill. Without it, you couldn't organize information in a logical way.

A Cross out the word that does *not* belong in each group.

1. **history words** era ancestors ligament serf industrial

2. **math words** multiple factor suburb subtract measure

3. **computer words** terminal debug cursor mouse tariff

4. **science words** cell biosphere predator preamble atomic

5. **geography words** tally planet erosion crater savannah

6. **literature words** prose urban dialogue fictional sonnet

B Classify the words in the box. Write each word under the correct heading. You will not use all the words in the box.

artery	skull	plain	poverty	humidity
femur	biceps	scapula	arson	tardiness
mountain	battery	perjury	valley	persona

BONES   **LANDFORMS**   **CRIMES**

_____   _____   _____

_____   _____   _____

_____   _____   _____

C Write a heading for each category. Then add one more item to each list.

_____   _____   _____

1. trout   1. honesty   1. sprint
2. salmon   2. loyalty   2. high jump
3. halibut   3. kindness   3. relay race
4. _____   4. _____   4. _____

Science class offers many opportunities to develop your classification skills.

A

Read each group of words. Decide what the words have in common. Then write a word from the box to complete the group. Use a dictionary if you need help with unfamiliar words. *Hint:* You will *not* use all the words in the box.

squids	sharks	fleas	ticks	butterflies	larva
turtles	panda	hippo	seals	salamanders	asps

1. egg, _____, pupa, adult

2. scorpions, _____, mites, spiders

3. lice, _____, bees, termites

4. snakes, _____, lizards, crocodiles

5. frogs, _____, toads, newts

6. adders, _____, cobras, rattlers

7. clams, _____, snails, oysters

8. whales, _____, porpoises, walruses

B

Carefully read each incomplete statement. Then write the word from the box that makes the statement *always* true. *Do not use any word more than once.* Use a dictionary if you need help with unfamiliar words.

ounce	fluids	herbivorous	sun	tomato	onion	lake
quart	humans	carnivorous	ring	animals	snakes	pound

1. A pound of ice weighs the same as a(n) _____ of water.

2. No _____ have limbs.

3. No _____ is a fruit.

4. Many _____ are quadrupeds.

5. All _____ are bipeds.

6. All horses are _____.

7. All planets have a(n) _____.

8. All gases are _____.

The science of physics includes the study of heat. This lesson will introduce you to some basic facts about temperature measurement.

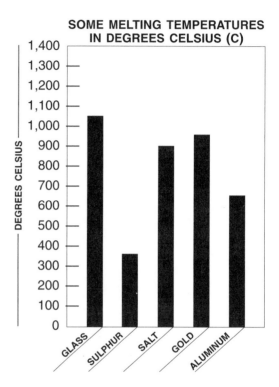

A

Study the bar graph on the right. Use the information to answer the questions.

1. _____ melts at about 1,050° C.

2. What compound or element on the chart melts at the *lowest* temperature? _____

3. What melts at about 660° C?

   _____

4. _____ melts at about 963° C.

5. At what temperature does salt melt? _____

The *Celsius* scale of temperature measurement was invented by Anders Celsius. He was a Swedish astronomer who lived from 1701 to 1744. On the Celsius scale, 0° is the freezing point and 100° is the boiling point of water.

Gabriel Daniel Fahrenheit, a German physicist, devised the temperature measurement scale that bears his name. On the Fahrenheit scale, 32° is the freezing point of water and 212° is the boiling point. Fahrenheit lived from 1686 to 1736.

B

Circle the words that correctly complete the sentences.

1. Although both inventors of temperature scales were scientists, (Celsius / Fahrenheit) was trained in studying the stars, while (Fahrenheit / Celsius) had studied energy and matter.

2. In the United States, the (Fahrenheit / Celsius) scale is used to measure air and body temperature, although most countries use the (Fahrenheit / Celsius) scale.

3. A normal body temperature of 98.6° F would be (37° / 24°) on the Celsius scale.

Read the handwritten letter. Notice that its author is Abraham Lincoln, the 16th president of the United States. If you visited Oxford University in England, you could see the original letter. Refer to lines in this letter to help you answer the questions on the next page.

> Executive Mansion
> Washington, Nov 21, 1864
>
> To Mrs Bixby, Boston, Mass,
>
> Dear Madam.
>
> 1   I have been shown in the files
> 2   of the War Department a statement of the Adjutant
> 3   General of Massachusetts that you are the mother of
> 4   five sons who have died gloriously on the field of battle
> 5   I feel how weak and fruitless must be any word of
> 6   mine which should attempt to beguile you from the
> 7   grief of a loss so overwhelming. But I cannot refrain
> 8   from tendering you the consolation that may be found
> 9   in the thanks of the republic they died to save. I
> 10   pray that our Heavenly Father may assuage the anguish
> 11   of your bereavement, and leave you only the cherished
> 12   memory of the loved and lost, and the solemn pride
> 13   that must be yours to have laid so costly a sacrifice
> 14   upon the altar of freedom.
>
> Yours very sincerely and respectfully
> A. Lincoln

Answer the questions in complete sentences.

1. When and where was this letter written? *Extra credit:* Do you
   know what war was being fought at that time?

   _____

   _____

2. To whom is the letter addressed, and where did that person live?

   _____

   _____

3. How did Lincoln know about the events that affected Mrs. Bixby?

   _____

   _____

4. What had happened that inspired the president to write to her?

   _____

5. What words in line 5 describe Lincoln's feelings about his
   message of condolence?

   _____

6. In lines 7 and 8, what does the president offer Mrs. Bixby?
   Rephrase his statement in your own words.

   _____

   _____

7. What words in lines 10 and 11 express Lincoln's prayer that
   Mrs. Bixby's sadness will be lessened?

   _____

   _____

8. In line 12, what phrase refers to Mrs. Bixby's sons? In lines
   13 and 14, what does Lincoln say Mrs. Bixby has done?

   _____

   _____

HISTORICAL TIMELINES

World War I and World War II were crucial events in American history. Study the timelines to improve your understanding of "what happened when."

 A

Write your answers in complete sentences.

1. Which came first—Germany's sinking of the *Lusitania* or the United States' entry into the war?

   _____

2. Was Germany defeated *before* or *after* Russia signed a peace treaty with Germany?

   _____

3. Was the Treaty of Versailles signed *before* or *after* Archduke Ferdinand was assassinated?

   _____

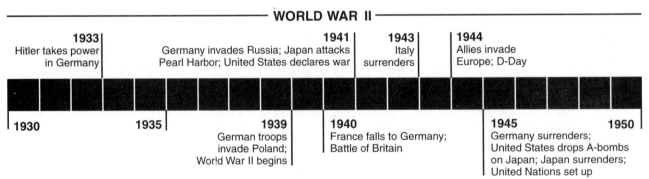

 B

Circle a word or a date to correctly complete each sentence.

1. Hitler rose to power (seven / eight) years before France fell to Germany.
2. German troops invaded (France / Poland) in 1939.
3. Japan attacked the U.S. Navy base at Pearl Harbor in (1943 / 1941).
4. World War II began (before / after) the Allies invaded Europe.

TWO PLANS FOR GOVERNMENT 14

Our founding fathers created America's first national government in 1781. This document was called the Articles of Confederation. By 1787, Americans had become dissatisfied with the Articles. They wanted a stronger national government. The Constitution we abide by today was signed on September 17, 1787. Use the information in the chart to compare the two documents.

THE ARTICLES OF CONFEDERATION AND THE CONSTITUTION

UNDER THE ARTICLES

- Congress could not collect taxes. If the country needed money, it had to ask the states for it.
- Congress could not control trade among the states or between states and other countries.
- Both the states and Congress could print money.
- It was difficult for Congress to make new laws because at least nine of the 13 states had to agree.
- Congress could not enforce its laws. If a state broke a law, there was nothing the government could do.
- Congress could only *ask* the states for men and money to defend the nation. The states could say no.
- It was difficult to change the Articles of Confederation because all of the states had to agree to any changes.

UNDER THE CONSTITUTION

- Congress can collect taxes to raise money needed by the nation.
- Congress can control trade between the states and with other countries.
- Only Congress can print money. The states can no longer print their own.
- Congress can make a new law if a *majority,* or more than half, of the Senate and of the House agree.
- The Constitution calls for a president to enforce the laws and a court system to try cases if laws are broken.
- Congress can raise an army and navy to defend the nation.
- The Constitution can be changed if two-thirds of Congress and three-fourths of the states agree to the change.

Show how the Constitution solved each problem in the Articles. Draw a line from each problem statement on the left to the Constitutional solution on the right.

1. Congress could not raise money.

2. Money in some states was worthless.

3. It was very difficult to change the Articles.

4. The states would not do what Congress ordered them to do.

5. The union could not defend itself.

a. The president makes sure that the laws are followed.

b. Congress can tax people.

c. Congress can draft people into the army.

d. If 2/3 of Congress and 3/4 of the states agree, the Constitution can be changed.

e. Only Congress can print money.

15 — LATITUDE AND LONGITUDE

Have you ever noticed the pattern of intersecting lines on maps? These lines that mapmakers draw are called lines of *latitude* and *longitude*.

What's the purpose of latitude and longitude?

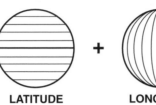  +  =

LATITUDE   LONGITUDE

THIS PATTERN MAKES IT POSSIBLE TO LOCATE ANY PLACE ON EARTH.

- Lines of latitude, or *parallels*, run east and west.
- Lines of latitude begin at 0° (zero degrees), the *equator*.
- Locations from the equator to the North Pole are referred to as *north latitude*. Locations from the equator to the South Pole are referred to as *south latitude*.

- Lines of longitude, or *meridians*, run north and south.
- Lines of longitude begin at 0° (zero degrees), the *prime meridian*.
- Locations from 0° to 180° east of the prime meridian are referred to as *east longitude*. Locations from 0° to 180° west of the prime meridian are referred to as *west longitude*.

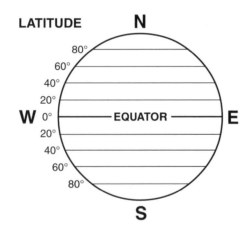

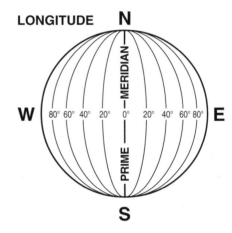

A

Fill in the blanks to complete the sentences.

1. Both the prime meridian and the _____ are located at 0°.

2. Locations between the equator and the _____ Pole are referred to as south latitude.

3. Lines of longitude can also be called _____.

4. Lines of latitude are sometimes called _____.

B

Study the map of South America. Then answer the questions.

1. How many degrees apart are the lines of latitude and longitude on this map?

_____

2. The equator runs through which three South American countries?

_____

_____

_____

3. Which city is located at about 23° south latitude, 44° west longitude?

_____

4. Which city is located at about 35° south latitude, 59° west longitude?

_____

5. Give the location in latitude and longitude for the city of Caracas, Venezuela.

_____

_____

6. Suppose you're on a ship anchored in the harbor of Montevideo. Give the location of your ship in latitude and longitude.

_____

_____

7. Is Buenos Aires east or west of Santiago?

_____

8. Give the location in latitude and longitude for the city of Santiago, Chile.

_____

_____

9. Is Peru north or south of the equator?

_____

Can you reach the island where the pirate treasure is buried? Follow the directions.

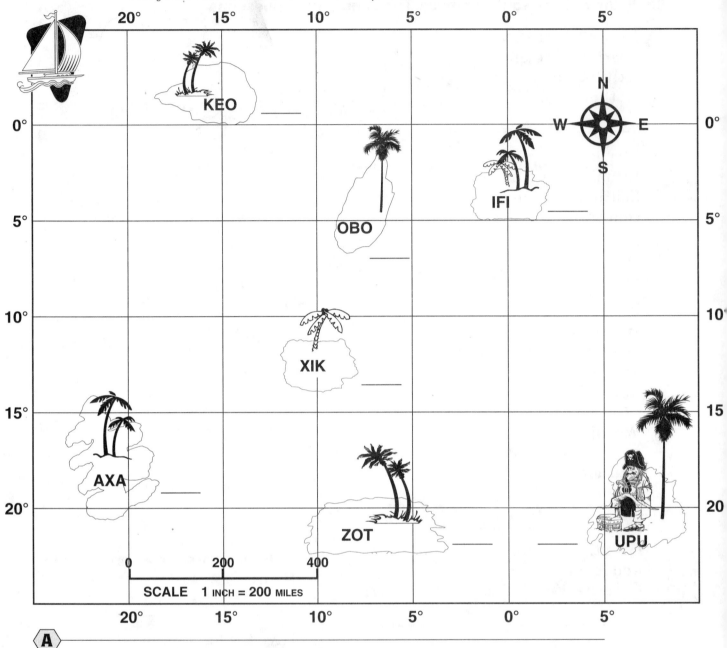

A

As you reach each location, write a number on the line. Then, as you sail along, connect your numbers with dotted lines.

1. Start your journey on the island located 15° south latitude, 20° west longitude. (Write the number 1 there.)

2. Sail to the island that is near the equator at 15° west longitude. (Write the number 2 there.)

3. Sail on to the spot on the ocean that is 10° south latitude, 10° west longitude. (Write the number 3 there.)

4. Now sail straight east until you reach 5° west longitude. (Write the number 4 there.)

5. From this point you sail in a northeasterly direction until you land at 5° south latitude on the prime meridian. (Write the number 5 there.)

6. When you leave there, sail southward until you land at 20° south latitude, 5° east longitude.

CONGRATULATIONS! You found it!

B

Use the scale at the bottom of the treasure map to help you fill in the blanks or answer the questions.

1. The scale shows you that 1 inch on the map equals how many miles? _____

2. The distance between AXA and KEO is _____ miles.

3. How far is it from KEO to the location you marked with the number 3?_____

4. You sailed about _____ miles to get from number 3 to number 4.

5. From there to IFI was a voyage of about _____ miles.

6. When you left IFI, you still had about _____ miles to go before you found the treasure.

7. In all, how many miles had you sailed? _____

8. If you had traveled *directly* from AXA to UPU, you would have sailed _____ miles.

● ● ● ● ● ● ● ● ● ● ● ● ● ● ● ● **JUST FOR FUN** ● ● ● ● ● ● ● ● ● ● ● ● ● ● ● ● ● ●

FOLLOWING DIRECTIONS

1. Place your pencil in the middle of the white circle.

2. Now go out Exit 2.

3. When you reach the first black circle, go out Exit 7.

4. At the intersection, make a turn and follow Route 9.

5. Stay on Route 9 until you reach the next circle. Leave on Exit 10.

6. At the intersection, turn and follow Route 14.

7. When you reach the next circle, go out Exit 17.

8. Follow Route 17 carefully, and soon you'll be OUT!

Did you know that a majority of popular votes will *not* automatically win a presidential election? A president's election is official only when Congress counts the votes of the Electoral College on January 6. When a nominee gets *one* more than half of the total of electoral votes, the race is over.

Electoral Votes for President (538 total votes)

The Constitution allows each state to cast as many electoral votes as it has representatives in Congress. Because each state has two senators and at least one representative in the House of Representatives, no state has fewer than three electoral votes.

⬡ A

Study the information on the map. Then circle a letter to show how each sentence should be completed.

1. The states with the *fewest* electoral votes are Alaska, Wyoming, North Dakota, South Dakota,

   a. Mississippi, and Alabama.

   b. Vermont, and Delaware.

   c. Connecticut, and New Hampshire.

2. The state with the *greatest* number of electoral votes is

   a. Texas.   b. New York.   c. California.

3. The number of representatives a state sends to Congress is based on that state's

   a. population.   b. location.   c. wealth.

4. It makes sense that presidential nominees spend much of their time campaigning in

   a. Washington, D.C.   b. the larger states.   c. the Midwest.

When George Washington was elected, there were just 13 states and only 69 electoral votes. The number of electors in each state is still determined as it was in Washington's time. Many people are critical of the Electoral College system for these reasons:

1. There is no guarantee that an elector who is pledged to vote for a certain candidate will actually do so. (A few electors have switched their votes—but none has ever changed the outcome of an election!)

2. The winner-take-all system seems unfair. A nominee can get *all* of a state's electoral votes by getting just *one* more popular vote than his or her opponent. (Because of this rule, three nominees have been elected president even though their opponents received more popular votes nationally.)

B

Use the information on both pages of this lesson to answer the questions or complete the sentences.

1. How many electoral votes does a nominee need to win the presidency?

   _____

2. What are the five states with the greatest number of electoral votes?

   _____

   _____.

   In total, how many votes do these five states have? _____

3. In 1824, Andrew Jackson received more popular votes than John Adams, yet lost the _____. The vote was so close that neither _____ won the _____ of the electoral votes. The decision then went to the House of _____, which elected _____.

4. In nearly all states, electors are _____ to cast their electoral votes for the nominee who received the most _____ votes in that state.

Riddles and puzzles are an enjoyable way to practice following directions.

A

Use the clues to solve the riddles.

1. If you change two letters in the word *joke*, you'll find me in an egg.

   _____

2. I'm a round object that represents the world. Take away one letter and I am part of your ear. _____

3. I'm a large bird with a beautiful tail. Take away my last syllable and I become a vegetable. _____

4. I like to climb trees and eat bananas. When you take away my first syllable, I can open a lock. _____

5. I am round, light, and colorful as I float in the air. Take away my last three letters, and I can bounce. _____

6. I like to snack on your clothes. Add two letters and I become a very important person. _____

B

Read the clue to each word. Then write the answer words in order from top to bottom. The last letter of each *preceding* word begins the new word. Each new word has one more letter than the preceding word. The first word has been filled in.

1. opposite of yes   *no* _____

2. nocturnal bird   _____

3. opposite of first   _____

4. wild animal   _____

5. tool for tennis   _____

6. home on wheels   _____

7. let go; set free   _____

8. remove water; let dry   _____

9. coming to an end   _____

10. identity with birth country   _____

Can you follow very detailed directions? Skill at following directions
is important for success at school as well as in later life.

 C

**Read each numbered instruction *carefully*. Then follow the directions
below the boxes. Check your work when you're finished.**

Box 1	57	64	35	25	98	
Box 2	P	Q	R	S	T	U	V
Box 3	man	coat	run	jump		

1. In box 1, circle the number that is equal to (6 x 6) minus 1. In box 3, circle the second letter of the third word.

2. Circle the middle letter in box 2, the first letter of the fourth word in box 3, and the number equal to (5 x 5) in box 1.

3. Put a cross on the letter before *S* in box 2. Draw a circle around the number equal to (10 x 10) minus 2 in box 1. Then draw a circle around the second vowel in the second word in box 3.

4. Put a circle around the last consonant in the last word in box 3. Then draw a cross on the number in the fifties in box 1.

5. Put a circle around the letter after *U*. Make a cross on the letter before *Q* in box 2. Put a circle around the first word in box 3. Make a cross on the last letter of the second word. Finally, put a cross on the number equal to (8 x 8) in box 1.

 D

**Study the numbered instructions. Then carefully follow the
directions. Check your work.**

1. Is the number of circles equivalent to the number of squares and triangles? If so, put a *dot* in the last circle.

2. Is the number of triangles preceding the four letters equal to the number of circles in the box? If so, put a *cross* on the third letter in the box.

3. Are there three consecutive figures—each one different from the others—in the box? If so, *circle* the third consecutive figure.

4. Is the number of letters equal to the number of digits in the box, and do digits follow letters? If so, put a dot in the first square.

5. Do two consecutive digits added together equal the third digit? If so, put a dot in the second square.

OBJECTS AND ACTIONS

Can you accurately match an object with its action? These analogies test your understanding of "what does what."

EXAMPLES: object to action: *Broom* is to *sweep* as *mop* is to *wash* .

action to object: *Fly* is to *kite* as *cook* is to *stove* .

smell	damage	tongue	fingers	bond
pliers	bray	nozzle	swing	howl
kick	touch	foot	hammer	accident
pound	nose	glue	wolf	bleat

⬢ Follow the directions. Try to use each word only once.

1. Choose one object and the action that matches it from words in the box. Write the words on the lines.

    OBJECT: _____   ACTION: _____

2. Complete each analogy with a word from the box.

    a. *Chew* is to *teeth* as *taste* is to _____.

    b. *Top* is to *spin* as _____ is to *squirt*.

    c. *Cut* is to *scissors* as *grasp* is to _____.

    d. *Bee* is to *buzz* as *donkey* is to _____.

    e. *Pitcher* is to *pour* as *pendulum* is to _____.

    f. *Howl* is to *wolf* as _____ is to *sheep*.

3. Choose four words from the box to write an analogy relating *objects to actions*. Write your analogy on the line.

    _____

4. Choose four words from the box to write an analogy relating *actions to objects*. Write your analogy on the line.

    _____

A Cross out the word that *doesn't* fit in each category. Add the word to the category it *does* fit.

1. **motion   energy   matter   election** _____

2. **tail   diamond   aquamarine   ruby** _____

3. **sound   fins   scales   gills** _____

4. **ballot   opal   candidate   majority** _____

B Write **T** or **F** to show whether each statement below is *true* or *false*.

1. _____ A timeline is used to show the sequence of related events.

2. _____ Under the Articles of Confederation, only Congress could print money.

3. _____ On a globe, lines of longitude run east and west.

4. _____ A state has one Electoral College vote for each member it has in the House of Representatives.

5. _____ The United States was involved in World War II from 1914 to 1919.

6. _____ The Fahrenheit temperature scale is used in most countries around the world.

C Circle a word or words to correctly complete each sentence.

1. Abraham Lincoln's letter to Mrs. Bixby would be classified as a message of (congratulations / condolence).

2. An appropriate heading over the words *teal, rust, charcoal,* and *amber* would be (colors / types of ducks).

3. Lines of longitude and latitude show the (population / location) of all the world's major cities.

4. Distances between the lines of latitude and longitude on a globe are measured in (scales / degrees).

READING AT SCHOOL II

FOR HELP WITH THE LESSONS, SEE THE GLOSSARY OF TERMS, PAGES 110–112.

UNIT
3

19 — **UNIT PREVIEW**

A

Where did we get the alphabet we use today? You can find out by numbering the paragraphs *in sequence*.

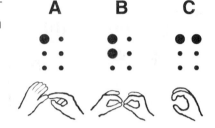

Slowly, over hundreds of years, the idea of the alphabet spread. People who spoke many different languages began using marks to stand for the sounds of their languages.

Long before they could read or write, people wanted a way to help them remember things. They wanted to be able to send messages. First, they tried drawing pictures. It was easy to draw pictures for words like **sun**, **man**, or **baby**. But pictures did not work well for words like **but**, **go**, **all**, or **understand**.

The English learned the Roman alphabet from the Romans who came to England. The Roman alphabet did not have all the sounds of the English language. That's why the English sometimes used two Roman letters to stand for one sound. **Th** stands for a sound that the Romans did not use.

When English people came to America, they brought the English language and the Roman alphabet with them. The alphabet we use today is still called the Roman alphabet.

The Romans were one of these peoples. They made an alphabet that had all the sounds of their language. When Romans went to England, they took their alphabet with them.

Then someone had a better idea than drawing pictures. The idea was to make a mark for every sound that was in a word. We don't know who this person was. We don't know what language he or she spoke. But this idea was the beginning of our alphabet.

Almost from the beginning, human beings have known how to talk. Before they learned to read or write, everything they knew had to be learned by heart. They could not send messages.

B

Write *T* or *F* to show whether each statement below is *true* or *false*.

1. _____ The terms *in sequence* and *chronological order* are synonyms.

2. _____ The key word that led you from paragraph one to paragraph two was *message*.

3. _____ Before people drew pictures, they probably were already communicating with hand signals and simple speech.

4. _____ It would be easy to draw a picture to represent a word like *nevertheless*.

SEQUENCE

It's hard to understand anything if its parts are out of order. Learning to *recognize* correct sequence is an important thinking skill. Learning to *create* sequence is even more useful!

A The *boldfaced* letters are out of sequence. Unscramble the words and write them on the lines. Then write the answer to each question.

1. What is your **ANEM** _____? _____

2. Are you a **LAME** _____

   or a **FLAMEE** _____? _____

3. What is your **DSERDSA** _____?

   _____

4. Are you having a **PAYPH** _____ day?

   Write **ON** _____ or **EYS** _____   _____

B The words in these sentences are out of order. Rewrite the words in proper sequence.

1. letters alphabet first of the are the seven *d, c, g, b, f, e, a.*

   _____

   _____

2. period one years a millennium of is thousand a.

   _____

   _____

3. between the 19 and 22 numbers 23 and 21 are 20.

   _____

   _____

C Number the words below to show chronological order.

1. _____ sophomore   _____ senior   _____ freshman   _____ junior

2. _____ cool   _____ roll out dough   _____ eat cookies   _____ bake

Have you ever completely forgotten an important appointment? Have you accidentally planned two activities for the same time? Writing out your schedule on a monthly calendar can help you stay organized!

A

As you take time to think ahead, the month of May will be especially busy for you. Make brief notes on the calendar to remind you of important dates listed below. To save space, use abbreviations, initials, or symbols if you like.

- Your final exam in math class is May 24.
- May 3 is your best friend's birthday.
- Notice that Mother's Day is May 14 this year!
- You have tickets for a concert on May 18.

- Grandma needs a ride to the doctor's on May 11.
- You have a baby-sitting job the second Tuesday in May.
- You're getting a haircut on May 4.
- When should you make a campground reservation for Memorial Day weekend?

MONTHLY PLANNER — MAY

SUNDAY	MONDAY	TUESDAY	WEDNESDAY	THURSDAY	FRIDAY	SATURDAY
	1	2	3	4	5	6
7	8	9	10	11	12	13
14 MOTHER'S DAY	15	16	17	18	19	20
21	22	23	24	25	26	27
28	29 MEMORIAL DAY	30	31			

A *weekly* calendar helps you focus on tasks that must be accomplished in a period of seven or five days. Notice that the calendar below provides spaces for workdays only.

 B

First write the abbreviated date over each day (September 1, for example, should be abbreviated 9/1). Then write at least one reminder for each morning and afternoon. Jot down the exact *hour* for each event, appointment, or deadline.

THIS WEEK				
Mon. _____	Tues. _____	Wed. _____	Thurs. _____	Fri. _____
A.M.	A.M.	A.M.	A.M.	A.M.
P.M.	P.M.	P.M.	P.M.	P.M.

On *very* busy days' you may need to list your tasks in order of importance. The job that has *top priority* is the one that must be done first. Tasks that could be put off until the next day should be at the bottom of the list.

C

Use the *daily* planner to organize the listed tasks *in order of priority*. To help you decide, ask yourself, "What would the consequence be if I didn't get this done today?"

- Bathe the dog.
- Study for tomorrow's history test.
- Think about a future career.
- Cancel tomorrow's dentist appointment.
- Pick up little sister after school.
- Deliver newspapers at 7 A.M.
- Hang around with my pals.
- Write Uncle Pete a thank you note.

TODAY'S TASKS

DATE _____ FINISHED ✔

1		☐
2		☐
3		☐
4		☐
5		☐
6		☐
7		☐
8		☐
9		☐
10		☐
11		☐
12		☐

Are you a fan of detective stories? Read about the talented American writer who invented this favorite form of fiction.

A

Study the information in the article. Then circle a letter to show how each sentence should be completed.

The first detective stories were written more than 150 years ago by Edgar Allan Poe. Although he was an American, Poe set these stories in Paris, France. The hero of his detective stories was a Frenchman, C. Auguste Dupin.

In Poe's work as a magazine editor, he came to understand what the public wanted to read—spine-tinglers! His first detective story, called *The Murders in the Rue Morgue*, was about a baffling series of murders. The police knew that the killer seemed to have superhuman strength. But only the clever Dupin was able to figure out that the murderer was in fact a giant ape.

Another Dupin story, *The Purloined Letter*, was about blackmail in high society. When the police failed in their search for the stolen letter, they again turned to the amateur detective Dupin. With Dupin's help, they located the letter and brought the blackmailer, a cabinet minister, to justice.

In his own day, Poe was most famous as a poet and a critic. Over time, however, he became recognized as a master of the short story who influenced many later writers.

1. Edgar Allan Poe lived about
   a. 350 years ago.
   b. 150 years ago.
   c. 100 years ago.

2. The main idea of this article is that Poe
   a. was a well-known poet.
   b. lived in the 19th century.
   c. wrote the first detective story.

3. One detail in this article tells you that
   a. Poe was an American.
   b. Poe died by drowning.
   c. Poe preferred writing poems.

4. "Spine-tinglers" are stories that
   a. inspire the reader.
   b. frighten the reader.
   c. warm the reader's heart.

5. A synonym for the word *purloined* must be
   a. blackmail.
   b. forged.
   c. stolen.

6. To "bring someone to justice" must mean
   a. to see that the wrong-doer is punished.
   b. to give a stern warning.
   c. to grab him by the neck.

7. The article mentions that later storytellers
   a. copied Poe's work.
   b. learned from Poe's work.
   c. disregarded Poe's work.

8. This article is made more interesting by
   a. details of Poe's personal life.
   b. examples of Poe's plots.
   c. the physical description of Dupin.

Edgar Allan Poe is regarded as one of the most important American authors of the 19th century. Today he is remembered for his poetry as well as his popular tales of horror. Few writers have ever come close to achieving his dramatic power and emotional intensity.

Read the events from the short and troubled life of Edgar Allan Poe. Then rewrite them on the lines _in sequence_ (from first to last).

- In 1837, Poe goes to Philadelphia to work as a magazine writer.

- In 1809, Edgar Allan Poe is born.

- In 1847, Virginia Clemm dies of tuberculosis.

- In 1829, Poe is expelled from West Point for heavy drinking.

- In 1849, Poe dies after a bout of heavy drinking.

- In 1812, Poe's parents, who are traveling actors, die.

- In 1845, Poe works as a reporter on New York's _Evening Mirror._

- In 1836, Poe marries his 13-year-old cousin, Virginia Clemm.

1. _____

2. _____

3. _____

4. _____

5. _____

6. _____

7. _____

8. _____

22 — SYLLOGISMS

A *syllogism* is a special form of reasoning. In a syllogism, two statements are made and a logical conclusion is drawn from them. The first statement in a syllogism is called its *major premise*. The second statement is the *minor premise*, and the third statement is the *conclusion*.

EXAMPLE: major premise: **All mammals are warm-blooded.**

minor premise: **Whales are mammals.**

conclusion: **Therefore, whales are warm-blooded.**

A

Read the syllogisms below. Then write a word or letter to correctly complete the conclusion.

1. All men are mortal.

   Socrates is a man.

   Therefore, Socrates is _____.

2. A is exactly the same as B.

   B is exactly the same as C.

   C is exactly the same as _____.

3. The red box is bigger than the green box.

   The green box is bigger than the blue box.

   The red box is bigger than the _____ box.

B

Think about the information given in each pair of sentences. Is there enough information to draw a logical conclusion? Answer each question by circling *Yes*, *No*, or *We don't know*. If you answer *We don't know*, explain why. Tell what information is missing or which word makes a conclusion impossible.

1. Everyone in Mike's class likes Mike. Vernon is in Mike's class. **Does Vernon like Mike?**

   Yes.   No.   We don't know.

   _____

2. Every girl in the Juarez family wore a white dress last Sunday. Martha is one of the Juarez girls. **Did Martha wear a white dress?**

   Yes.   No.   We don't know.

   _____

3. Everyone over ten years old in Mrs. Smith's family is more than five feet tall. **Is Bob Smith more than five feet tall?**

   Yes.   No.   We don't know.

   _____

4. All the children in the second grade weigh more than 40 pounds. Arlene is in the second grade. **Is it possible that she weighs 35 pounds?**

   Yes.   No.   We don't know.

   _____

5. All drivers stop their cars before they cross Main Street. Mr. Jones drove his car across Main Street. **Did Mr. Jones stop his car before he crossed the street?**

   Yes.   No.   We don't know.

   _____

6. Every intersection downtown has either a stop sign or a red light. **Does the corner of Broad and Elm have a stop sign or a red light?**

   Yes.   No.   We don't know.

   _____

7. Everyone in the seventh grade except Jim wore boots to school today. **Does Jim have a pair of boots at home?**

   Yes.   No.   We don't know.

   _____

8. Most children like ice cream. Mary is a child. **Does Mary like ice cream?**

   Yes.   No.   We don't know.

   _____

23 THE VOCABULARY OF LITERATURE

The study of literature has its own vocabulary.

Read the six literary terms and definitions. Then read the lists of examples, and write the term that matches.

event: an occurrence; something that happens

moral: the instructive point of a story

novel: a long form of fiction with a complex plot

theme: the central meaning or subject of a story

mood: the overall feeling the author creates in a story

conflict: the struggle between characters or forces at the center of a story

1. man against the weather
   brother against brother
   good self vs. bad self
   _____

2. revenge
   everlasting love
   ambition
   _____

3. *Two Years Before the Mast*
   The Hunchback of Notre Dame
   The Three Musketeers
   _____

4. Honesty is the best policy.
   Two wrongs don't make a right.
   Biggest is not always best.
   _____

5. lighthearted
   gloomy
   suspenseful
   _____

6. plane crash
   wedding
   arrival of a stranger
   _____

Complete each sentence with a word from the box. *Hint:* **You will *not* use all the words.**

setting	narrator	introduction	fiction	author
symbol	dialogue	characters	description	plot

1. _____ are the fictional people who play

   parts in a story or novel.

2. The _____ is the writer of a story, poem,

   novel, or any other written composition.

3. The _____ is the location and time the story

   takes place.

4. Words that tell about the appearance of the setting and the characters are called _____.

5. A story's _____ is the chain of events that leads to its outcome.

6. Sometimes an author will use a _____ to represent an important underlying idea.

7. Words spoken by characters in a story or play are called _____.

8. The _____ is the character who tells the story in his or her own words.

9. A literary work in which the plot and characters come from the author's imagination is called _____.

C

Use the clues to help you solve the crossword puzzle. Answers are words from Part B.

ACROSS

5. The characters' _____ was very clever and funny.
6. Jim Hawkins is the _____ of *Treasure Island*.
8. The _____ of *Dr. Jekyll and Mr. Hyde* is 19th century London.
9. The author's _____ of the battle scene was bloody and gruesome.

DOWN

1. Scrooge is one of the world's best known story _____.
2. A war novel's _____ is usually packed with action.
3. *A Tale of Two Cities* is a famous work of historical _____.
4. Mark Twain is a much-loved American _____.
7. In *Moby Dick*, the white whale is a _____ of evil.

A

Read the famous lines from literature. Circle a letter to show the meaning of each quotation. Then label each famous line with its source. Write the correct author and title from the box. *Hint:* You will *not* use all the authors and titles.

Stephen Crane	*The Adventures of Huckleberry Finn*
Daniel Defoe	*Carrie*
Charles Dickens	*A Christmas Carol*
Stephen King	*Frankenstein*
Herman Melville	*Moby Dick*
Mary Shelley	*The Red Badge of Courage*
Mark Twain	*Robinson Crusoe*
H. G. Wells	*The War of the Worlds*

1. *"Bah," said Scrooge. "Humbug!"*

   a. Take your bugs and leave.
   b. I want no part of such foolishness.
   c. Celebrating holidays is great fun.

   AUTHOR: _____ TITLE: _____

2. *"My name is Ishmael. A whale-ship was my Yale College and my Harvard."*

   a. My professor went whaling, too.
   b. Classes were held aboard ship.
   c. I learned everything I know at sea.

   AUTHOR: _____ TITLE: _____

3. *"There warn't no home like a raft, after all. Other places feel so cramped up and smothery, but a raft don't."*

   a. Life on the river is scary and lonely.
   b. Life in town is too confining.
   c. Most homes are way too small.

   AUTHOR: _____ TITLE: _____

4. *"I beheld the wretch—the miserable monster whom I had created."*

   a. I was pleased with my creation.
   b. I couldn't believe how ugly he was.
   c. He was exactly as I expected.

   AUTHOR: _____ TITLE: _____

5. *"Henry was going to look at war, the red animal—war, the blood-swollen god."*

   a. Henry was chasing a red animal.
   b. Henry feared being wounded or killed.
   c. Gunpowder made smoky red clouds.

   AUTHOR: _____ TITLE: _____

6. *"I was exceedingly surprised with the print of a man's naked foot on the shore."*

   a. Someone had come to kill me.
   b. Wearing shoes was not optional.
   c. I realized I was not alone on the island.

   AUTHOR: _____ TITLE: _____

B

Circle a word to correctly complete each sentence.

1. From the line, *"My name is Ishmael,"* you can tell that Ishmael will be the story's (**author** / **narrator**).

2. The line, *"I beheld the wretch,"* tells you that the narrator of the story is (**speaking** / **listening**).

3. Scrooge's (**description** / **dialogue**) tells you that he is cranky and mean.

4. The person who sees someone's footprint on the shore is one of the story's (**characters** / **symbols**).

5. The (**dialogue** / **setting**) of the person on a raft shows a lack of education.

6. The author of the war story uses the color red as a (**symbol** / **description**) for blood.

7. "Cramped up" and "smothery" are words of (**character** / **description**) used by the boy on the raft.

8. The (**plot** / **setting**) of the whaling story is no doubt at sea.

• • • • • JUST FOR FUN • • • • • •

Fact or fantasy?

1. Draw a triangle if the school cafeteria serves *gourmet* food. →

2. Draw a rectangle if the school secretary helps the principal. →

3. Draw a circle if English is an *extracurricular* activity. →

EXPLORERS OF THE NEW WORLD

Some 500 years ago, there was no such thing as an accurate map of the world. How much do you know about the *Age of Exploration*?

Study the information in the chart. Then circle a letter to answer each question.

EXPLORERS OF THE NEW WORLD				
NAME	NATIONALITY	FLAG	MAIN ACHIEVEMENT	DATES
John Cabot	Italian	English	North Atlantic voyager	1497
Pedro Cabral	Portuguese	Portuguese	explored Brazil's coast	1500–1501
Jacques Cartier	French	French	sailed up St. Lawrence River in Canada	1534–1536
Christopher Columbus	Italian	Spanish	first European to reach New World	1492
Hernando Cortez	Spanish	Spanish	conquered Mexico	1519
Sir Francis Drake	English	English	first Englishman to make voyage around the world	1577–1580
Ferdinand Magellan	Portuguese	Portuguese	led first voyage around the world	1519–1522
Francisco Pizarro	Spanish	Spanish	discovered Peru	1513

1. Which nations laid claim to lands in Mexico and South America?

    a. England and France

    b. England and Spain

    c. Italy and Portugal

    d. Spain and Portugal

    e. France and Portugal

2. Which explorer on the chart could be called a *conqueror*?

    a. Jacques Cartier

    b. Sir Frances Drake

    c. Ferdinand Magellan

    d. John Cabot

    e. Hernando Cortez

3. Which nation laid early claims in Canada?

    a. Spain

    b. Portugal

    c. England

    d. Italy

    e. France

4. Who led the very first voyage around the world?

    a. Christopher Columbus

    b. Sir Frances Drake

    c. Ferdinand Magellan

    d. John Cabot

    e. Francisco Pizarro

5. Which two explorers made the *earliest* voyages?

    a. Pizarro and Magellan

    b. Drake and Pizarro

    c. Cabot and Columbus

    d. Columbus and Cabral

    e. Cortez and Cabral

6. About how many years ago did an explorer first reach Peru?

    a. nearly 400 years

    b. nearly 500 years

    c. about 600 years

    d. about 550 years

    e. less than 200 years

B

Use information in the chart—and your own thinking power—to identify the explorer. Write a name on each line.

1. He led five ships on a historic expedition to find a new sea route to Asia. Three years later, one ship returned to Spain. It was the first ship to go around Cape Horn and cross the Pacific Ocean.

   This explorer was _____.

2. He was born in Genoa, Italy, of English parents. At the age of 34, he left Italy and settled in Bristol, England. He started his expedition when reports claimed that Columbus had found the westward passage to India. As he sailed along the New England coast, he believed that he had reached northeastern Asia.

   This explorer was _____.

3. King Emanuel of Portugal appointed him commander of a trading expedition to India. Before reaching India, the 13 vessels under his command sailed the coast of South America. He claimed possession of the region for Emanuel.

   This explorer was _____.

4. After joining Velasquez in the conquest of Cuba, this explorer went on to invade the Aztec empire. After tearing down the Aztecs' capital city, he built Mexico City on its ruins. Although his conquest resulted in riches for Spain, he was responsible for great cruelty to the Aztecs.

   This explorer was _____.

26 INVENTIONS

Certain inventions had a major impact on the way people work and live. Read the name of each invention and the date it was invented.

- **dynamo 1831**
- **spinning jenny 1764**
- **telephone 1876**
- **steam-powered loom 1785**
- **telegraph 1837**
- **steamboat 1807**
- **cotton gin 1793**
- **water frame 1769**
- **flying shuttle 1733**
- **steam locomotive 1804**

A

Study the inventions and dates above. Then rewrite the list in *chronological order* by beginning with the first invention.

INVENTION   DATE   INVENTION   DATE

1. _____ _____   6. _____ _____

2. _____ _____   7. _____ _____

3. _____ _____   8. _____ _____

4. _____ _____   9. _____ _____

5. _____ _____   10. _____ _____

B

Now fill in the timeline to show the correct date of each invention.
As an example, the *dynamo* has already been written in the timeline.

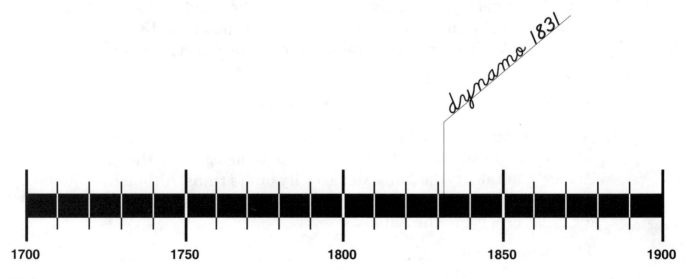

1700   1750   1800   1850   1900

Read the paragraphs. Then write the name of an invention on each line.

1. The _____ was the first machine to convert mechanical energy into electrical energy. Its invention was made possible by Michael Faraday's discovery of the principle of electromagnetic conduction.

2. Eli Whitney's _____ separates fibers from seeds. Before its invention, the removal of seeds was a tedious process that could only be done by hand.

3. The invention of the _____ by British inventor John Kay greatly increased the speed of the hand loom. With this mechanization, one person (instead of several) could accomplish the third step in the process of weaving fabric.

4. The _____ came into general use by the early 1900s. Although it essentially resembled the hand loom, this invention added several accessory devices that streamlined the weaving process.

5. Samuel Morse's _____ used a simple code to transmit messages by passing electrical impulses over a single wire. The first version of this invention resembled a simple electrical switch. Its signals could only be transmitted about 20 miles.

6. The _____ had smooth wheels operating on smooth metal rails. First used only in mining operations, it was later modified by another British engineer to pull cars carrying passengers and freight.

7. The basic unit of the first _____ consisted of a transmitter, a receiver, and a single connecting wire. Current generated by a battery traveled through a wire to the receiving station. There, vibrations reproduced the sound made into the transmitter.

8. Robert Fulton's invention of the _____ revolutionized power-driven navigation. This vessel became famous by making a 150-mile trip in 32 hours. Before Fulton's invention, the same trip took a sailing sloop four days to complete.

SEQUENCE AND DEGREE

Two standard types of analogies are those that use words to relate *sequence* (before or after) and those that use words to relate *degree* (more or less).

EXAMPLES: **sequence:** *Six* is to *four* as *ten* is to _eight_ .

Write is to *edit* as *seedling* is to _tree_ .

degree: *None* is to *some* as *few* is to _many_ .

Better is to *good* as *sweeter* is to _sweet_ .

law	sprinkle	last	everything	stew
64	happiest	infant	vegetables	rain
68	diamond	fossil	toddler	more
first	molehill	nothing	mountain	bill

◆ Follow the directions. Try not to use a word more than once.

1. Choose two words from the box to complete the relationships shown below. Write the words on the lines.

    sequence: *cloud* is to _____

    degree: *happier* is to _____

2. Complete each analogy with a word from the box.

    a. *Calf* is to *cow* as *dinosaur* is to _____.

    b. *Gale* is to *breeze* as *torrent* is to _____.

    c. *Worse* is to *worst* as _____ is to *most*.

    d. Number *11* is to *22* as number *34* is to _____.

    e. *Introduction* is to *conclusion* as *coal* is to _____.

    f. Number *90* is to *81* as number *73* is to _____.

3. Choose four words from the box to write an analogy relating *sequence*. Write your analogy on the line.

    _____

4. Choose four words from the box to write an analogy relating *degree*. Write your analogy on the line.

    _____

A. Unscramble the words to name six flowers. Write the letters in *sequence*.

1. **LYIL** _____
2. **LIPUT** _____
3. **SORE** _____
4. **CRODHI** _____
5. **SIDAY** _____
6. **PAINTUE** _____

B. Write the *conclusion* of these syllogisms.

1. Summer is hot.
   July is a summer month.

   _____

2. Tom is tall.
   Roger is taller.

   _____

C. Is each statement *true* or *false*? Write **T** or **F**.

1. _____ Edgar Allan Poe is best known for his short stories.

2. _____ *Chronological order* and *order of priority* are different words for the same thing.

3. _____ A story's *plot* is the time and place it happens.

4. _____ Herman Melville is the author of *Moby Dick*.

5. _____ *Mix*, *pour*, and *bake* are cake-making steps listed in sequence.

6. _____ The flying shuttle made it much easier to separate seeds from fiber.

D. Use the clues to complete the crossword puzzle with names of famous explorers and inventors.

ACROSS

1. Italian citizen who explored under the English flag
3. Inventor of the steamboat
4. Discoverer of Peru
5. Inventor of the telephone
6. First Englishman to complete an around-the-world voyage

DOWN

1. Conqueror of Mexico
2. Inventor of the telegraph
3. Inventor of the dynamo

READING IN THE COMMUNITY

FOR HELP WITH THE LESSONS, SEE THE GLOSSARY OF TERMS, PAGES 110–112.

UNIT
4

 UNIT PREVIEW

 A

Circle a letter to show the *most likely* explanation for each situation described.

1. The busiest hour at the Post Office service counter is from noon to 1 P.M.

   a. Morning is a bad time to buy stamps.

   b. Workers do chores on their lunch hour.

2. Your neighborhood library reduces its hours. Now it's only open five hours a day and one night a week.

   a. Library funding has been cut.

   b. The librarian is busy with her new baby.

3. The Recreation Department is hiring many temporary workers for three months.

   a. All permanent workers are taking long vacations.

   b. Recreation centers need extra help in summertime.

 B

Think about these places in your community. Then cross out the word that you would *not* be likely to hear in each place.

1. **library**

   overdue   reference   postage   nonfiction

2. **polling place**

   fine   ballot   candidate   election

3. **community center**

   schedule   classes   fee   license

4. **bus terminal**

   departure   route   transfer   flight

5. **shopping mall**

   retail   clerk   merchandise   violation

Many skills are involved in understanding what you read. Simply *paying attention* is the most important. That only makes sense. If your mind is on lunch or next Friday night's dance, the words in front of you won't mean much. How can you arrive at a sound conclusion or form a reasonable opinion if your thoughts are elsewhere?

A Read the passage about reading comprehension. Pay close attention to the **boldfaced** words.

GETTING MEANING FROM A MESSAGE

First, **scan** the paragraph, page, or chapter in order to **classify** the form and type of the written piece. Is it a letter, an essay, or a set of instructions? Is it fiction or nonfiction? Is the author trying to inform, to explain, or to persuade? Then **determine** the central idea. Once you **identify** the main idea, **observe** the details. Next, take a few moments to **recall** anything you already know about the subject. Try to **generalize** from your prior learning. This will often help you **interpret** the new information. To make sure you got the facts straight, **conclude** by quickly reading through the passage one more time.

B Use the definitions to help you complete the puzzle. Answers are the **boldfaced** words from Part A. The mystery word (reads from top to bottom) names "the act of using reasoning to reach a conclusion or form an opinion."

1. to form a broad idea from particular facts
2. to reach a decision after thinking
3. to sort out; to arrange by category
4. to see, watch, or notice
5. to explain the meaning of
6. to remember
7. to point out, locate, or recognize
8. to look over quickly
9. to finish or bring to an end

1. __ __ __ __ __ __ __ __ __
2. __ __ __ __ __ __ __ __ __
3. __ __ __ __ __ __ __ __
4. __ __ __ __ __ __ __
5. __ __ __ __ __ __ __ __
6. __ __ __ __ __ __
7. __ __ __ __ __ __ __
8. __ __ __ __
9. __ __ __ __ __ __ __ __

It can be hard to find a street address if you don't know the neighborhood. Do you know how to read a street map? Read the explanation and look at the example.

Notice the letters along the top of the map and the numbers down the left side. These letters and numbers divide the map into squares. The *street index* on a city map refers you to one or more of these squares. Read the example street index. Notice that the name of each street is followed by a letter-number pair. If two or more pairs are listed, the first pair shows where the street *begins*, and the second pair tells where the street *ends*.

EXAMPLE:

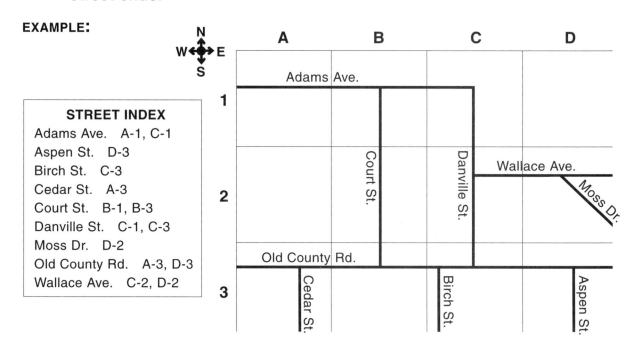

STREET INDEX
Adams Ave.   A-1, C-1
Aspen St.   D-3
Birch St.   C-3
Cedar St.   A-3
Court St.   B-1, B-3
Danville St.   C-1, C-3
Moss Dr.   D-2
Old County Rd.   A-3, D-3
Wallace Ave.   C-2, D-2

Study the map and the index. Then circle the words that correctly complete the sentences.

1. From this section of a street map, you can see that Danville Street runs (north and south / east and west.)

2. The intersection of Adams Avenue and Court Street is located in square (B-1 / C-1).

3. Adams Avenue appears in (two / three) squares on the map.

4. Old County Road begins in A-3 and ends in (D-4 / D-3).

B

Now use the map below to locate each street listed in the index. Write the letter-number pair for each street. If a street begins in one square and ends in another, write a letter-number pair for *both* ends of the street.

STREET INDEX

1. Ames Avenue,

   _____

2. Broad Street,

   _____

3. Cherry Street,

   _____

4. Grant Street,

   _____

5. Lincoln Street,

   _____

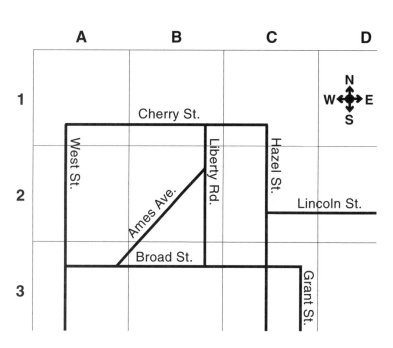

C

Write a street name, a direction, or a letter-number pair to correctly complete each sentence.

1. Liberty Road runs north and south

   between Cherry Street and _____.

2. _____ runs east and west, beginning at Hazel Street.

3. _____ intersects with Liberty Road in square B-3.

4. If you are driving _____ on Hazel Street, you must

   turn left to get onto Lincoln Street.

THE AIRPORT

The airport is busy this afternoon. Several passengers are checking this monitor.

AM-SKY

DEPARTURES

TIME	FLIGHT NO.	GATE	TO	COMMENTS
4:40	551	A10	Denver	Boarding
4:51	407	A15	Chicago	Delayed
5:02	599	B1	Toledo/Detroit	On Time
5:18	91	A4	Los Angeles	On Time
5:30	902	B17	Denver	On Time
5:45	810	B9	Phoenix	Canceled

A

Use information on the monitor screen to complete the sentences.

1. The information on this monitor tells only about flight _____, not about arrivals.

2. Kyla is going to Chicago. She sees that her flight, No. _____, will board at Gate _____.

3. Johnny starts to run. His fellow passengers are already taking their seats on Flight No. _____.

4. This afternoon's flight to _____ leaves at 5:18.

5. It is now 4:40, and Kathy has just stepped up to the ticket counter. Luckily, she can still catch the plane to Chicago because that flight has been _____.

6. The last flight to Denver boards at Gate _____.

7. Flight No. 599 is scheduled to leave on time at _____
   for _____ and _____.

8. Passengers who hoped to be in Phoenix tonight will be disappointed
   to see that their flight has been _____.

9. Between 4:40 and 5:45 there are _____ flights
   scheduled to take off.

AM-SKY

ARRIVALS

TIME	FLIGHT NO.	GATE	FROM	COMMENTS
8:30	201	40	Salt Lake City	Delayed
8:59	309	5	Raleigh	On Time
9:38	124	34	New York	On Time
9:52	7811	11	Buffalo	Delayed
-----	-----	-----	-----	-----
-----	-----	-----	-----	-----

B

Study the information on the monitor. Then write _T_ or _F_ to show whether each statement below is true or false.

1. _____ Mrs. Le's flight from Raleigh is scheduled to arrive at 9:38.

2. _____ Rod can meet his granddad's plane from Buffalo at Gate 11.

3. _____ The flight from Salt Lake City will be early because of a gate change.

4. _____ Brittany will be on time to meet the flight from New York if she gets to the gate by 9:30.

30 — BUS ROUTE MAP

Do you know how to get around town
on public transportation?

**The bus company's *route map* shows you where each bus
goes. Notice that each route has its own number. Study the
route map below.**

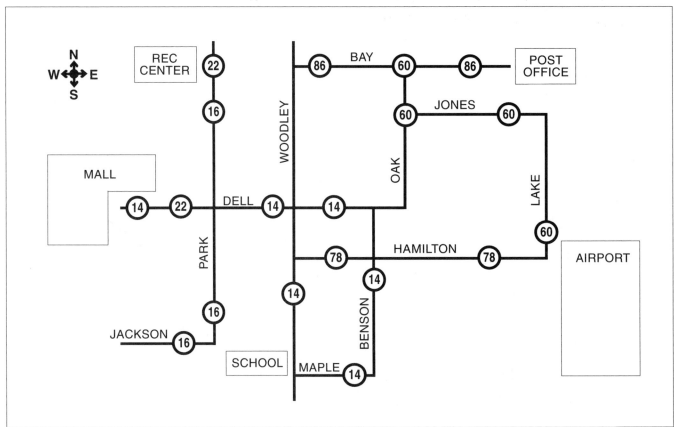

A

Circle a letter to answer each question.

1. Which bus travels *only* east and west?

    a. 22   b. 14   c. 78

2. Which two bus routes lead to the mall?

    a. 16 and 22   b. 14 and 22   c. 60 and 14

3. Which bus route runs by the school?

    a. 14   b. 78   c. 16

66

4. How many bus routes travel back and forth on Dell?
   a. one   b. three   c. two

5. Bus route 14 covers which three streets?
   a. Dell, Benson, Maple   b. Oak, Jones, Lake   c. Oak, Dell, Park

B

Use the route map on the facing page to help you answer the questions.

1. Freddie is at the corner of Maple and Benson. He wants to go to the corner of Park and Dell. What bus should be take? _____

2. George is at the mall. What bus will take him to the recreation center? _____

3. Selena is at the corner of Oak and Jones. Which bus should she take to the airport? _____

4. Wendy has a package to mail. She lives on Woodley, near Bay. Which bus will take her to the Post Office? _____

Sometimes, passengers must take two or more buses to get to their destination. When they change buses along the way, they *transfer* to a different route.

C

Find places on the map where passengers could transfer from one route to another. Circle the word that correctly completes each sentence.

1. To get from school to the recreation center, Laura will transfer from bus 14 to bus (16 or 22 / 16 only).

2. After working at the mall, Paco will transfer from bus 14 to bus (78 / 60) to get to his home on Lake.

3. To get from the airport to his home on Jackson, Roy will make his first transfer onto route (14 / 78) and his final transfer onto route (22 / 16).

31 — THE MALL

Do you and your friends like to meet at the mall?

Study this *floor map* of a shopping mall.

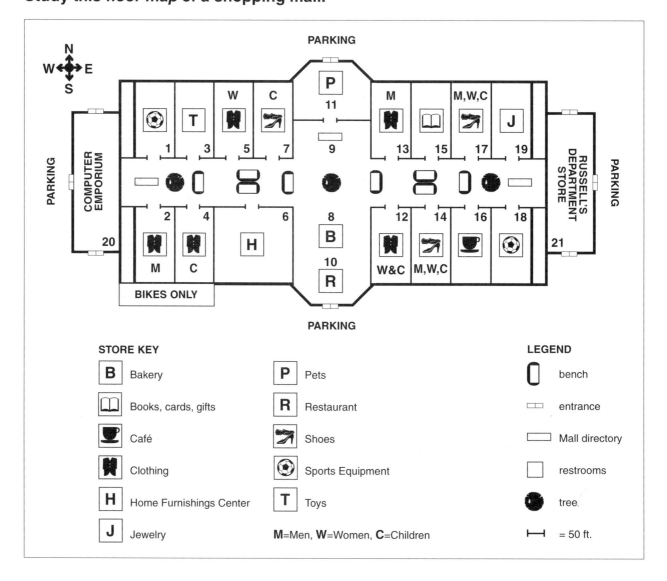

Answer the questions or circle words to correctly complete the sentences. Use the information in the map to help you.

1. If you were directing someone to the pet store, you could say that it was (at the end / in the middle) of the mall on the (south / north) side.

2. Is there a camera store in this mall? _____

31

3. In which store could you find modems, monitors, and software?

   _____

4. The key under this map lists (exits and entrances / kinds of stores).

5. How many stores in this mall sell clothing? _____

6. If you parked in the east parking lot, you would enter the mall
   through (Russell's Dept. Store / Computer Emporium).

7. Can you enter the mall directly from the south parking lot?

   _____

8. You can find the location of restrooms in the (legend / key).

9. Is there a health food store in this mall? _____

10. The bookstore is located in which space number? _____

11. What store is directly across from the children's shoe store?

    _____

12. If you needed a lamp for your living room, what two stores might you
    visit? _____ and

    _____

13. The (sporting goods store / bakery) is located at the center of the
    mall on the south side.

14. You will pass (three / two) stores as you walk from the jewelry store
    to the men's clothing store.

15. According to the scale in the legend, it's about (700 / 7,000) feet from
    the mall's south entrance to its north entrance.

32 VOTING RIGHTS

One of an American's most precious rights is the right to vote. How much do you know about voting laws?

In the United States, a person has to meet only four requirements in order to vote. The law requires that a voter must:

1. *Be a United States **citizen**.* All persons born in the United States are U.S. citizens. A person born in a foreign country whose parents are U.S. citizens is also a citizen. A person who is not a citizen can become a naturalized citizen. First, however, he or she must meet certain requirements: must have lived in the United States for five years and be at last 18 years old; must be able to read, write, and speak English; must understand the Constitution and promise to uphold it; and must take a test about U.S. history and government.

2. *Be at least 18 years old.* This age was set by the 26th Amendment, passed in 1971. Before that time, 21 was the voting age in most states.

3. *Have lived in the area where he or she intends to vote* for some time. Usually the requirement is 30 days. States have this rule so that only local people can vote in local elections.

4. ***Register** before voting* (in every state except North Dakota). To register, a person must give his or her name, address, age, and other facts to an election official. Then the voter's name gets added to the list of other voters in your state. States first started registering voters to keep them from voting twice.

It is against the law for anyone to take away a person's right to vote because of sex, race, background, or religion. A person cannot be stopped from voting because he has little money or does not own land. It is also against the law for anyone to use force of threats to stop or change a person's vote.

A person can lose the right to vote in some cases. Most states take away the voting rights of people who have been found guilty of serious crimes. The right to vote can also be taken away from people who are gravely mentally ill.

A

Use the information in the box and your own knowledge to choose the best ending for each sentence. Circle a letter to indicate your choice.

1. Two kinds of citizens who would not be allowed to vote are
   a. a jaywalker and a rapist.
   b. an insane person and a murderer.
   c. a six-year-old and a very old man.

2. When citizens register to vote, they declare themselves either independents or members of a political party. Some political parties in the United States are
   a. Liberal, Conservative, and Radical.
   b. Whig, Tory, and Federalist.
   c. Republican, Democrat, and Libertarian.

3. It is important that only local people can vote in local elections because
   a. others have no stake in the outcome.
   b. outsiders are unwelcome.
   c. others can't travel that far.

32

4. The article says that states register voters to keep them from voting twice. What other purpose(s) are served by voter registration?

    a. Each political party can keep track of its membership.
    b. States can ensure that all voters meet the requirements.
    c. both a. and b.

5. If you don't bother to vote, you

    a. are committing a federal crime.
    b. save time for more important activities.
    c. lose your say in how you are governed.

B

Use the clues and the information in the box to complete the crossword puzzle.

ACROSS

4. To become a naturalized citizen, a person must _____ to uphold the Constitution.
6. Before 1971, 21 was the legal voting _____ in most states.
8. It is illegal to deny people's voting rights because of their _____.
9. People who want to be citizens must pass a test about American _____.

DOWN

1. About 30 years ago, an _____ to the Constitution lowered the voting age.
2. It is illegal for anyone to try to change your _____.
3. The government requires that every voter must be a _____.
5. You must be able to read, write, and speak English to vote in an _____.
7. States _____ voters to keep them from voting twice.

••• JUST FOR FUN •••••

What has a bed but never sleeps?

Each sentence gives you a clue to a letter. Answer the riddle by putting the letters together.

1. _____ My first letter is in *tired,* *but* not in *diets.*
2. _____ My second letter is in *relieve,* but not in *lever.*
3. _____ My third letter is in *driver,* but not in *drearier.*
4. _____ My fourth letter is in *primer,* but not in *primary.*
5. _____ My fifth letter is in *shriek,* but not in *sheik.*

I am a _____.

Crossword grid:
- 1 A
- 2 V
- 3 C
- 4 P
- 5 E
- 6 A
- 7 R
- 8 R
- 9 G

71

ROCKLAND COMMUNITY CENTER
Schedule of Fall Classes

- **Senior Fitness**
  Low-impact exercise for you who are 60+. Wear comfy clothes.
  M-W-F   10–11 A.M.   8 wks. $25

- **Beginning Guitar**
  No exp. req. Get started making music. Fun class.
  T-Th   8–10 P.M.   12 wks. $65

- **Intermediate Square Dancing**
  Must know basic steps. Join in the fun.
  Th   8–10 P.M.   12 wks. $65

- **Pumping Iron**
  Develop a personalized weightlifting program. Adults only.
  M-W-F   7–9 P.M.   8 wks. $35

- **Wonders of Nature**
  Sunday afternoon nature hikes w/ informative naturalist. Learn as you walk! All ages.
  4 wks. $20

- **Advanced Ceramics**
  Must have taken Intermed. course. $15 materials fee.
  W   7–10 P.M.   8 wks. $45

- **Slim Swim**
  Tone up underwater! Look better, feel great.
  M-Th   noon to 1 P.M.   10 wks. $40

- **Be a Clown!**
  Beginning circus act techniques for children 8–12.
  Sat   10–noon   10 wks. $45

- **Gymnastics for Tots**
  Healthy play for kids 2–4 yrs. old. Parent participation req.
  M-W-F   9–10:30 A.M.   10 wks. $40

- **Camera Club**
  Learn the secrets of fine portrait photog. 35mm camera req. Min. age 12 yrs.
  T   7–10 P.M.   12 wks. $75

A

Use information in the class schedule to help you complete the sentences or answer the questions.

1. Which class meets over the lunch hour on Mondays and Thursdays?

   _____

2. The *least* expensive class on this schedule is _____

   _____.

3. It (would / would not) be possible for you to take *both* the guitar class and the photography class.

4. Mr. and Mrs. Rossi hope to do their grocery shopping while their toddler is in gym class. Will that plan work? _____

5. (Advanced Ceramics / Camera Club) has an extra charge for materials you'll use in class.

6. The most expensive course offered on this schedule is

_____.

7. What class could an adult gymnast take to help stay in shape?

_____

8. It would cost ($115 / $100) to take *both* Intermediate Square Dancing and Pumping Iron.

9. Which two classes are given on weekends only? _____
_____ and _____

10. A 63-year-old who works weekdays from 9 to 5 (could / could not) take the Senior Fitness class.

B

Circle a letter to show the meaning of the *boldfaced* words.

1. a **personalized** weightlifting program
   a. a personable, friendly instructor
   b. tailored to your own needs
   c. a class for one person only

2. **low-impact** exercise
   a. lots of bouncing and jumping
   b. without hitting or punching
   c. not much stress on ankles and knees

3. **parent participation** required
   a. You must have a note from your parents.
   b. Parents must help out.
   c. Parents must wear gym clothes.

4. **adults only**
   a. no students under 18 years old
   b. ages 50–60 only
   c. only registered voters

34 — Driver's License

Different states have different requirements for licensing young drivers. The information below is taken from the California driver's manual.

MINOR'S REQUIREMENTS TO GET A PROVISIONAL DRIVER'S LICENSE

- You must be at least 16 years old.

- You must prove that you have completed both driver education and driver training.

- You must have had an instruction permit for at least six months.

- You must provide a parent's signature on your instruction permit saying you have completed 50 hours of supervised driving practice, 10 hours of which were completed at night.

- You must pass the behind-the-wheel driving test. If you fail the test, you must wait two weeks before being tested again. You have three chances to pass the driving test within the time your permit is valid.

- You must get a thumbprint.

- You must have your picture taken after you pass your driving test.

A

Use your own prior learning, common sense, and information on the chart to help you correctly complete the sentences.

1. The term *driver education* means (classroom / behind-the-wheel) training.

2. To get (an instruction permit / a driver's license) you must have had 50 hours of supervised driving practice.

3. Students under 18 years of age are issued (regular / provisional) driver's licenses.

4. Instructors of driver training classes are licensed by the (state / city).

5. A provisional license allows you to drive alone as long as you are not involved in (gang activity / a traffic accident).

6. Your photo and thumbprint are both used to (identify / supervise) you as a licensed driver.

7. You must apply for an instruction permit (before / after) you apply for a driver's license.

8. A person under 16 (does / does not) qualify for a provisional driver's license.

STUDENT DRIVER

9. If you fail the behind-the-wheel driving test, you must wait for (two / three) weeks before taking it again.

10. At least 10 hours of supervised night driving is (requested / required) to get a driver's license.

B

What are the facts about teenagers and driving? Use your best judgment to show how each sentence on the left should be completed. Write a letter on each blank.

1. _____ When you violate traffic laws, you

2. _____ As a group, teenagers average

3. _____ Nearly half of all drivers under 19

4. _____ Many new drivers have accidents

5. _____ The most common violation for teenage drivers

6. _____ If you are ill, sleepy, or upset about something,

a. is speeding.

b. you are taking a risk if you attempt to drive.

c. increase your chances of having an accident.

d. twice as many accidents as adult drivers.

e. are convicted of a traffic violation in their first year of driving.

f. at intersections.

PARTS AND WHOLES

Is a *shoe* part of a *sole* or is a *sole* part of a *shoe*? The analogies below show the relationships between whole things and parts of things.

EXAMPLES: part to whole: *Knuckle* is to *finger* as *lobe* is to *ear* .

whole to part: *Belt* is to *buckle* as *sandal* is to *strap* .

seam	teeth	handle	sentence	violins
blood	wick	flower	spoon	crystal
word	spark	piston	stanza	ice
deck	stitch	card	molar	orchestra

◆ Follow the directions. Try not to use a word more than once.

1. Choose a *part* and a *whole* that it matches from the words in the box. Write them on the lines.

    whole: _____ **part:** _____

2. Complete each analogy with a word from the box.

    a. *Camera* is to *lens* as *candle* is to _____.

    b. *Beard* is to *whisker* as *bouquet* is to _____.

    c. *Oxygen* is to *air* as *hemoglobin* is to _____.

    d. *Room* is to *ceiling* as *engine* is to _____.

    e. *Wave* is to *ocean* as _____ is to *fire*.

    f. *Chapter* is to *novel* as _____ is to *poem*.

3. Choose four words from the box to write an analogy relating *parts to wholes*. Write your analogy on the line.

    _____

4. Choose four words from the box to write an analogy relating *wholes to parts*. Write your analogy on the line.

    _____

Ⓐ Write **T** or **F** to show whether each statement is *true* or *false*.

1. _____ To interpret information means to locate it on the page.

2. _____ A map of the United States always has a street index.

3. _____ A monitor at the airport shows whether flights are on time or delayed.

4. _____ Restroom locations are shown on the floor map of a mall.

5. _____ Letter-number pairs help you locate streets on a city map.

6. _____ Bus companies change route numbers every day.

Ⓑ Circle the word that correctly completes each analogy.

1. *Flour* is to *dough* as *droplet* is to (*faucet* / *cloud*).

2. *House* is to *wall* as *fence* is to (*post* / *gate*).

3. *Bookshelf* is to *library* as *store* is to (*building* / *mall*).

Ⓒ Use the clues to complete the crossword puzzle. Answers are words you learned in this unit.

ACROSS

3. You sometimes have to _____ from one bus route to another.

4. the process of seating passengers on a plane

8. chart of upcoming events including days and times

9. You must learn about American _____ to become a U.S. citizen.

DOWN

1. common location of teenagers' traffic accidents

2. money charged for taking a class

5. lists street names on a city map

6. Symbols and abbreviations are explained in a map's _____.

7. The U.S. Constitution guarantees all adult citizens the _____ to vote.

READING IN THE MARKETPLACE

FOR HELP WITH THE LESSONS, SEE THE GLOSSARY OF TERMS, PAGES 110–112.

UNIT

5

35 — UNIT PREVIEW

A

Is it wiser to buy things with cash or on credit? Compare and contrast these two ways of making purchases. Write *pro* or *con* next to each statement to show whether it is an argument *for* or *against* using credit cards.

1. _____ You can make purchases over the telephone.

2. _____ You can take advantage of sale prices even if you don't have cash with you.

3. _____ You may buy more than you can afford without realizing it.

4. _____ You have to pay interest on the unpaid balance on your account.

5. _____ You have a way to pay for something in an emergency.

6. _____ You usually have to pay an annual fee of $25 or more.

7. _____ Your credit card bill is a record of your purchases.

B

Circle the word that correctly completes each sentence.

1. Classified ads for rental housing are filled with (accommodations / abbreviations).

2. Your credit limit is the (maximum / minimum) amount you are allowed to charge.

3. To figure out the total cost of shopping by catalog, you must include the (item numbers / shipping charge).

4. At 25% off, a suit that is regularly priced at $160 would sell for ($ 140 / $120).

5. Haste is often the (effect / cause) of waste.

COMPARING AND CONTRASTING

A Circle a letter to show how each sentence should be completed.

1. When you *compare* and *contrast* two things or ideas, you identify ways they are

    a. necessary or unnecessary.   b. alike and different.

2. To a buyer, important differences between two items of clothing might be

    a. lot number and packaging.   b. fit and durability.

3. The words *marketplace* and *workplace* both describe

    a. locations where a certain kind of activity takes place.

    b. specific street addresses in specific cities.

4. You might make a choice between two fast food items by comparing

    a. weight and color.   b. taste and price.

5. You might decide which of three used cars to buy on the basis of

    a. mileage and resale value.   b. weather and location.

B Write one way the items in each pair are alike and one way they are different.

1. **basketball, baseball**

    ALIKE: _____

    DIFFERENT: _____

2. **truck, van**

    ALIKE: _____

    DIFFERENT: _____

3. **adult, teenager**

    ALIKE: _____

    DIFFERENT: _____

Classified ads in the newspaper are a good place to look for rental housing. Notice how many words have been abbreviated (shortened) to save space.

1. Sm. studio exc. Downtown loc. $550 mo. 1st, sec. & clng. dep. req. Avail. 9/1. Call Jackie after 6 P.M. 555-2121

2. Country cabin 20 min. frm. town. Crprt, deck. Pets OK. Ref. & clng. dep. req. Avail. now. Call 555-9876

3. Lux. twnhse. Prestige loc. $2000 mo. 4 BR, 3 BA. Grt. view. 1st, last & sec. dep. Get app. at rental off. 200 Park Ave. 9-5 P.M.

4. Garden apt. 2 BR, 1 BA, AEK. New cpts. No pets, smkrs. or drugs. 1 yr. lease. $800 mo. Lv. msg. 555-0011

5. Lge. BR in my home. Shre kitch & lndry. rm. Quiet stu. pref. $400 mo. Share util. Nice neighbhd. 555-6545

6. M or F roommate to share condo w/ bro. & sis. Sm. BR & priv. BA. Near univ. campus. No smkrs. Move in 9/1. $425 mo. Call Farhad 555-9978

Can you figure out what each abbreviation means? Write a word from the box next to the abbreviation it matches.

available	bedroom	downtown	luxury	cleaning	location
minutes	required	bathroom	private	security	apartment
utilities	student	smokers	office	carport	townhouse
kitchen	preferred	application	message	deposit	references

1. smkrs. _____

2. clng. _____

3. dep. _____

4. ref. _____

5. off. _____

6. min. _____

7. loc. _____

8. app. _____

9. crprt. _____

10. twnhse. _____

Circle a letter to show how each sentence should be completed.

1. Property owners usually require a cleaning deposit to prevent a renter leaving an apartment

   a. to move to another town or state.

   b. dirty or damaged.

   c. freshly painted and decorated.

2. If you don't own a car, it's important that you choose an apartment
   - a. next door to your parents.
   - b. near a car dealership.
   - c. near the bus line and a grocery store.

3. If you give lots of parties and like loud music
   - a. the studio is not the place for you.
   - b. any of these places would be fine.
   - c. you must move to an island.

4. A *luxury* townhouse in a *prestige* location is probably
   - a. in need of a lot of repair.
   - b. too expensive for someone starting out.
   - c. filled with fine furniture.

5. A dog owner with a car might be attracted to the place described in
   - a. ad no. 5.
   - b. ad no. 4.
   - c. ad no. 2.

6. You would have to call to find out how much the rent is for the
   - a. country cabin.
   - b. townhouse.
   - c. garden apartment.

7. If you are a college student with no car, you should probably check out
   - a. ad no. 3.
   - b. ad no. 6.
   - c. ad no. 5.

Use the clues to complete the crossword puzzle.

ACROSS

4. gas and electric power

6. people who will say that you are responsible and trustworthy

DOWN

1. a one-room apartment; combination living room and bedroom

2. for your own use; not shared

3. abbreviation for *all electric kitchen*

5. written agreement to rent at a certain rate for a certain period of time

CREDIT CARD STATEMENT

Do you use a credit card? Do you understand all the information on the monthly statement you receive?

☰ABC Bank☰

Account Name	Account Number	Closing Date
Tom Kelly	4123-6131-0023-06	9•30•99

Credit Information

Credit Limit	1,000
Unused Credit	857
Amount Over	0

Account Activity

Previous Balance	$200 -
New Activity	$ 40 -
Payments	$ 100 -
Finance Charge	$ 20.34
New Balance	$ 160.34
Minimum Payment	$ 10 -
Date Payment Due	10-31-99

Annual Percentage Rate:
20%

Make Payments to:
ABC Bank
P.O. Box 1010
Omaha, NE 68104

For Lost or Stolen Cards:
1-800-555-6124

Trans Date	Description	Posting Date	Charges	Payments
9•2	sporting goods	9•4	$ 40 -	
9•15	Payment	9•17		$100 -
9•30	Finance Charge	9•30	$ 20.34	

NOTICE: NO FINANCE CHARGE IF NEW BALANCE RECEIVED BY PAYMENT DUE DATE.

Total New Charges	60.34
Amount Past Due	$ 0 -
New Balance	$160.34

A

Use the information on the statement to help you answer the questions.

1. Your *credit limit* is the total amount of money you are authorized to charge on the credit card. What is Tom Kelly's credit limit?

   _____

2. What *annual percentage rate* does Tom pay? _____

3. If Tom loses his credit card, what should he do? _____

4. Suppose Tom worked overtime this month and has some extra money. To pay off his entire *balance,* he must pay _____.

5. The *finance charge* is the amount of interest owed on credit used. What is Tom's finance charge this month? _____.

6. This statement shows all activity on Tom's account from August 31 through what date? _____

7. Did Tom pay off his entire balance last month? _____

8. What is the *least* amount of money Tom can pay on his account this month? _____

9. How much of his *previous balance* does Tom still owe? _____

10. An extra charge is added if Tom is late making his monthly payment. Does this month's bill show a *"late charge"*? _____

B

Circle a letter to show how each sentence should be completed.

1. If Tom pays off his bill and does not use his card this month, he will
   a. exceed his credit limit.
   b. have no finance charge next month.
   c. change account numbers.

2. Tom's next payment is due
   a. on Sept. 30.
   b. immediately.
   c. by Oct. 31.

3. If Tom wanted to use *all* the credit still available on this account, he could charge
   a. $857.
   b. $1,000.
   c. $160.34.

4. From the information on this statement, it appears that Tom is using his credit card
   a. less often than he should.
   b. responsibly.
   c. much too often.

— # CATALOG SHOPPING

It's time to buy holiday gifts again! This year you just can't face the traffic jams and the crowded malls. You've marked the following listings in your favorite catalog.

■ **LEATHER COIN PURSE**
Fully lined, about 4½" wide; basic navy blue. Roomy pockets for folding money, driver's license, and keys.
ORDER NO.
10-41584   Orig. **14.00**. Now only **6.00**.

■ **U.S. PRESIDENTS JIGSAW PUZZLE**
Have fun and learn history at the same time! Colorful, sturdy; 1,000 pieces. Huge 24" x 30" finished size. A great gift!
ORDER NO.
10-70922   Orig. **18.00**. Now only **12.00**.

■ **PATCHWORK LEATHER HAT**
Handmade in Argentina. Popular snap brim for high style. Multicolor stitching—no two hats alike! Supple cowhide, one size fits all.
ORDER NO.
10-82521   Orig. **36.00**. Now only **24.00**.

■ **GIANT RING TOSS GAME**
Safe, challenging entertainment for grown-ups and kids alike! Sturdy rack is easy to assemble. Giant rings 18" in diameter. Lightweight carrying case.
ORDER NO.
10-34532   Orig. **11.00**. Now only **8.00**.

■ **DOUGHNUT BAKER**
Help your favorite dieter enjoy guilt-free treats! Heavy steel pan bakes 6 doughnuts at a time. 9" x 13" size. Mouth-watering recipe included. Cuts calories!
ORDER NO.
10-446902   Orig. **17.00**. Now only **12.00**.

■ **HANDY SLACK RACK**
Compact rolling rack hangs 12 pairs of slacks wrinkle-free! Sturdy metal; 27" x 20" x 14" overall size. Saves closet space! Assembly required.
ORDER NO.
10-6619038 Orig. **15.00**. Now only **12.00**.

A

Use information from the catalog listings to complete the sentences.

1. The *least* expensive catalog item is the _____,
   and the *most* expensive is the _____.

2. You may need a screwdriver to help you put together the _____
   _____ and the _____.

3. There are _____ recreational items and _____ practical,
   useful items in these listings.

4. If you order Item No. 10-70922, you will receive the _____
   _____.

B

Use the catalog listings and the information on the right to help you answer the questions.

1. You decide to order the jigsaw puzzle and the ring toss game for your niece and nephew. What is the *combined* price of those two products?

   _____

2. How much will the shipping charge be for that order?

   _____

3. You notice that you could buy the coin purse without adding to the shipping charge. You decide to get it for your girlfriend. What item number do you write down?

PACKING & SHIPPING CHARGES
to first ship-to address:

Orders up to $29.99:   add $5.00
$30.00 to $59.99:   add $6.50
$60.00 and over: add $8.50

OUR PROMISE TO YOU:

Daisy wants you to be happy with your purchases. Please feel free to return any item for exchange or full refund.

PHONE ORDERS:

Call us toll-free at
1-800-555-1155.

Please have catalog, order form, and credit card at hand.

Phone order hours (Eastern time):
Monday–Thursday: 9:00 A.M. to 8:00 P.M.
Friday: 9:00 A.M. to 6:00 P.M.
Saturday: 10:00 A.M. to 4:00 P.M.

   _____

4. Before you fill out the order form you take another look at the doughnut baker. That might be just the thing to satisfy your sister's sweet tooth! *Not* counting shipping, what is the total cost of the four products you've selected so far? _____

5. How much would shipping be for the puzzle, the ring toss game, the coin purse, and the doughnut maker? _____

6. If you got the leather hat for your mom and the slack rack for your dad, you could finish your holiday shopping right now! Together, how much do these two additional items cost? _____

7. If you order these last two items, does the shipping charge increase or stay the same? What is the total amount including shipping?

   _____

   _____

CATALOG ORDER FORM

A

Complete the catalog order form with the items you selected on the previous page. Print clearly. Make sure you follow all the directions.

Daisy COMPANY

Rush this order to:

Name: _____

Shipping Address: _____

_____

Phone Number: (_____) _____

E-Mail: _____

Ship to a different address:

☐ Alternate ship-to address

☐ Address Correction   ☐ Gift Address

To: _____

Address: _____

_____

Message: _____

Happy Holidays!
We pay all state and local taxes until January 1 –

	ITEM NO.	ITEM DESCRIPTION	QTY	ITEM PRICE	ITEM TOTAL
1					
2					
3					
4					
5					
6					
7					
8					
9					
		ADD EXTRA SHEET FOR ADDITIONAL ITEMS.			

ORDER BY PHONE (TOLL-FREE)
1-800-555-1155
ORDER BY FAX
1-800-555-6626

Thank you for your order!

☐ Check or Money Order enclosed. (Do not send cash.)
Charge: ☐ Visa ☐ MasterCard ☐ American Express ☐ Discover
Account Number

Exp. Date (req.): ___/___   Signature: _____

Subtotal	
Packing & Shipping	
Shipping to add'l address ($4 ea.)	
Gift Wrap ($3 per gift package)	
TOTAL ORDER	

B

Circle the word that correctly completes each sentence.

1. It is (not acceptable / acceptable) to send cash with your order form.

2. The Daisy Company (will / will not) ship a gift directly to your sister's address.

3. The Daisy Company (does / does not) charge extra for gift wrapping.

4. (You / The Daisy Company) will pay for the call if you order by phone.

5. If you order by phone, you must pay with a (check / credit card).

Car shoppers usually consider several different models before they make a decision. Study the information in the chart. Then circle a letter to show the correct answer to each question.

Feature	RODEO XEL	VENUS LE	MAGNA GX
engine	3.4L V6	2.3L 4 cyl.	2.4L 4 cyl.
automatic transmission	standard	optional - $800	optional - $800
4-wheel disc brakes	standard	not available	not available
anti-lock brakes	standard	optional - $600	optional - $499
roadside assistance	standard	not available	not available
TOTAL MSRP*	$19,985	$21,005	$20,207

* Price comparisons based on MSRP of comparably equipped models. Level of equipment varies.

1. How many different cars does this chart compare and contrast?
   a. 4   b. 3   c. 5

2. It would be reasonable to assume that **MSRP** means
   a. Mighty Sweet Road Performance.
   b. Manager's Special Rating Program.
   c. Manufacturer's Suggested Retail Price.

3. The car with the smallest engine is the
   a. Venus LE.   b. Rodeo XEL.   c. Magna GX.

4. Anti-lock brakes add $499 to the price of a
   a. Rodeo XEL.   b. Magna GX.   c. Ford truck.

5. In this chart, the words *standard* and *optional* are
   a. synonyms.   b. homonyms.   c. antonyms.

6. The most expensive car described on the chart is the
   a. Rodeo XEL.   b. Magna GX.   c. Venus LE.

7. The car with the most features and the lowest price is the
   a. Magna GX.   b. Rodeo XEL.   c. Venus LE.

Smart shoppers *think* before they buy. What factors do you usually consider before making a purchase?

A

Circle a letter to show how each sentence should be completed.

1. Is there more than a nickel's difference between a 25-cent candy bar and one that cost 30 cents? The cheaper item might cost less because it is

   a. bigger.　　b. smaller.　　c. delicious.

2. One package of socks costs $6.99. Another package costs $8.99. The less expensive package might not be a bargain if there are

   a. rips and tears in the package.
   b. too many packages unsold.
   c. fewer socks in the package.

3. Two watches look very much alike, yet one is priced at $9.99 and the other is priced at $19.99. You should check to see if the less expensive watch

   a. has a brand name and a guarantee.
   b. has been used.
   c. chimes on every hour.

4. Three important factors in comparing any products are

   a. color, fabric, and smell.
   b. size, quantity, and quality.
   c. time, money, and people.

5. A very low price sometimes means that a product

   a. is cheaply made and won't last long.
   b. is being given away by the store.
   c. has a very high mark-up.

● ● ● **JUST FOR FUN** ● ● ● ● ●

What keeps things out and runs around the yard, yet never moves?

Each sentence gives you a clue to a letter. Answer the riddle by putting the letters together.

1. _____ My first letter is in *safe,* but not in *save.*

2. _____ My second letter is in *search,* but not in *starch.*

3. _____ My third letter is in *grand,* but not in *grade.*

4. _____ My fourth letter is in *place,* but not in *plane.*

5. _____ My fifth letter is in *pearl,* but not in *parlor.*

I am a _____.

How would you solve the problem? Write *add*, *subtract*, *multiply*, or *divide* on the first line. Then solve the problem and write the answer on the second line.

1. The shoe store had a big Summer Clearance sale. On Saturday, Lou sold 32 pairs of sandals. On Sunday he sold 41 pairs. How many pairs did he sell in all?

   _____   _____

2. The department store clerk stocked the shelves with six boxes of towels. Altogether, there are now 144 new towels on display. How many towels were in each box?

   _____   _____

3. The cafe served breakfast to 39 customers. At lunch, 65 customers were served. How many more customers were served at lunch than at breakfast?

   _____   _____

4. On average, the jewelry store sells four rings a day. How many rings are sold in two weeks?

   _____   _____

5. Taylor bought a software program for $65.98. He gave the clerk $75.00. How much change did he get back?

   _____   _____

6. Danielle bought three toys each for her four nieces and nephews. At $5.50 per toy, how much did she spend?

   _____   _____

7. Andre's new tennis racket cost $49.95. His sister Patricia chose a racket from the sale table for $29.99. In all, how much did they spend?

   _____   _____

CAUSE AND EFFECT

...cognize which action or condition caused which result?
...alogies test your comprehension of *causes* and *effects*.

...ES: cause to effect: *Germ* is to *disease* as *accident* is to _damage_ .

effect to cause: *Snore* is to *sleep* as *answer* is to _question_ .

fatigue	celebration	birth	earn
insult	exercise	rain	stoke
fasten	investment	toil	burn
applause	puddle	fall	save

◆ Follow the directions. Try not to use a word more than once.

1. Choose one *cause* and the *effect* it matches from the words in the box. Write them on the lines.

   cause: _____ **effect:** _____

2. Complete each analogy with a word from the box.

   a. *Sneeze* is to *pollen* as *fitness* is to _____ .

   b. *Confidence* is to *compliment* as *discouragement* is to _____ .

   c. *Reach* is to *catch* as *slip* is to _____ .

   d. *File* is to *smooth* as *staple* is to _____ .

   e. *Death* is to *mourning* as _____ is to *celebration*.

   f. *Punishment* is to *crime* as *return* is to _____ .

3. Choose four words from the box to write an analogy relating *causes to effects*. Write your analogy on the line.

   _____

4. Choose four words from the box to write an analogy relating *effects to causes*. Write your analogy on the line.

   _____

A Circle words to correctly complete the sentences.

1. When you compare and contrast two products, you look for (substitutions / similarities) and differences.

2. An apartment ad that says *2 BR 1 BA* has two (bathrooms / bedrooms).

3. In a rental ad, the abbreviations *app.* and *off.* mean (application and office / appearance and official).

4. If you make a catalog order by fax or phone, you must supply the number of your (checking / credit card) account.

5. If your monthly payments are current, you will not see a (past due / finance) charge on your credit card statement.

6. A zero balance on your credit card statement means that you have no (available credit / unpaid debt).

B Use the clues to complete the crossword puzzle. Answers are words you learned in this unit.

ACROSS

1. A _____ card is handy in an emergency.

5. Renters must usually pay a cleaning _____.

6. Crime is the *cause* of _____.

7. To know if clothing will fit, you must check its _____.

8. Comparing the _____ of several cars can help you make a decision.

DOWN

2. To order from a catalog, include the product's _____ number.

3. Features that are not standard on a car are _____.

4. A credit card bill arrives _____.

6. Cars are often compared by the Manufacturer's Suggested Retail _____.

READING IN THE WORKPLACE

FOR HELP WITH THE LESSONS, SEE THE GLOSSARY OF TERMS, PAGES 110–112.

UNIT **6**

42 — UNIT PREVIEW

A

Circle a letter to show how each sentence should be completed.

1. You might find a good job lead in the newspaper by reading the
   a. sports section.   b. classified ads.   c. editorials.

2. A company's *policies* are its
   a. employee benefits such as health insurance.   b. full range of product parts.   c. official ways of operating.

3. The amount of money you receive when you cash a paycheck is your
   a. net pay.   b. withholding tax.   c. gross pay.

4. Another name for a *paycheck stub* is
   a. W-4 form.   b. earnings statement.   c. financial plan.

B

Use the clues to complete the crossword puzzle. Answers are job titles, workplaces, or job tasks.

ACROSS

2. An _____ connects parts to help manufacture a product.

4. A waiter or waitress is a _____ (2 words).

5. An _____ worker may type, file, and answer phones.

7. A place that sells plants, flowers, and trees is a _____.

DOWN

1. A route _____ delivers or picks up things in a certain part of town.

3. A gardener _____ and edges lawns.

4. A _____ buys wholesale flowers and arranges them for sale.

6. A _____ sells you goods in a retail store.

92

WORD ANALYSIS

First-time workers must be able to read and understand a lot of new information. Unfamiliar words can be a challenge. If you don't have a dictionary handy, you can often figure out the meaning of an unfamiliar word by studying its *parts*.

- A *compound word* is formed when two or more words are combined into one: *salesmen, workplace, downtown.*

- A *prefix* is a group of letters added to the beginning of a word to change its meaning: *cosign, resale, interact.*

- A *suffix* is a group of letters added to the end of a word to change its meaning: *agreement, instruction, respectfully.*

A Cross out the word in each group that is *not* a **compound word**.

1. withholding   newspaper   Social Security   warehouse

2. overtime   employees   paycheck   bookkeeper

B In each sentence, find a word with a *prefix*. Underline that word and then circle a letter to show its meaning.

1. Han's coworkers in the warehouse are Chip and Josh.

   a. bosses   b. fellow employees   c. assistants

2. There's no paper for the copy machine—it must be time to reorder office supplies.

   a. review an   b. remind someone   c. make another
   order   to order   order for

3. Benjamin's interview with the crew boss went very well.

   a. meeting to   b. casual chat   c. inside view
   discuss a job   between friends   of something

C In each sentence, find a word with a *suffix*. Underline that word and then circle a letter to show its meaning.

1. Nick needs full-time employment for the summer months.

   a. a certain   b. working without   c. the condition of
   kind of work   being paid   having a job

2. The company's new management cut unnecessary expenses.

   a. directors   b. attorneys   c. subcontractors

3. Kelly works as an assistant to the president's secretary.

   a. advisor   b. helper or aid   c. supervisor

Have you ever read employment ads in the classified section of the newspaper? Did you use context clues to help you figure out what the abbreviations mean?

ASSEMBLERS
Start. pay $6/hr. Must have gd. fing. coord. for fine wk. Temp. F/T pos. Only steady wkrs. need app. Intervws. Sat. 9 A.M.–noon. 1757 Kelly St.

CUSTOMER SERVICE REP
Entry lev. opp. for eager beaver! Trn. to adv. to mgmt. Off. loc. on bus line. (012) 555-1212

DISPATCH DRIVERS
P/T Th & Fri PM's. 2–10. Local rtes. Must have cln. driv. rec. $7 per hr. Call Monica (000) 190-0990.

FOOD SERVERS
P/T at excl. retiremt. hom. Grt 1st jb. for studs. Gd. pay. Will train. Bilingual a +. Call Jim or Nora 1 P.M.–5 P.M. 141-1100.

INVENTORY COUNTERS
No exp. nec. 18 yrs.+ Must have own rel. transp. Gd. wages. Bonus for fst. wrkrs. Call 999-0000.

OFFICE ASST.
P/T Wed-Th-Fri in busy machine shop. Must be comp. savvy & have gd. org. skills. Fax resume to Rita Vallejo, (000) 567-8923.

A

Write a letter to match each abbreviation with its meaning.

1. _____ **P/T**

2. _____ **Temp. F/T**

3. _____ **1st jb.**

4. _____ **excl.**

5. _____ **entry lev. opp.**

6. _____ **gd. fing. coord.**

7. _____ **REP**

8. _____ **rel. transp.**

a. entry level opportunity

b. Representative

c. part-time

d. good finger coordination

e. temporary full-time

f. first job

g. reliable transportation

h. exclusive

B

Complete the sentences with job titles from the ads.

1. The ad for a _____ offers training for advancement to a management position.

2. The retirement home needs _____ to help out at mealtimes.

3. If you want to be hired as a _____, you must have a clean driving record.

4. People who want to be _____ must apply in person on Saturday morning.

5. _____ who can work very quickly will be paid a bonus.

6. Good organizational skills are required for the _____ _____ job.

C

Write *T* or *F* to show whether each statement is *true* or *false*.

1. _____ If you got the customer service rep job, you wouldn't need a car to get to work.

2. _____ Excellent English skills are required for assembly work.

3. _____ Bilingual food servers could talk to older people who don't speak much English.

4. _____ You won't be hired as a dispatch driver if you've gotten several traffic tickets.

5. _____ When a warehouse takes inventory, every item in stock is counted and recorded.

6. _____ You must put together a résumé if you want to apply for the dispatch driver's job.

THE EMPLOYEE HANDBOOK

In many companies, a new worker will be given an *employee handbook* the first day on the job. Whether the handbook is a small pamphlet or an inch-thick paperback, the information it contains can be helpful to beginning employees.

Most employee handbooks contain at least three categories of information:

- **Introduction to the Company**

  This section describes the company's goals and purposes. It explains how the company operates and may include a *chart of organization* showing all company department heads from the president down. It might also contain a *flow chart* illustrating all the steps in manufacturing the company's product or providing its service. The history of the company could also be included in this section.

- **Company Policies and Procedures**

  A company's *policies* are its official ways of doing things. Policies regarding employees may include information about regular working hours and overtime, job performance standards, appropriate clothing for front office workers, rules regarding expense accounts for company travel, and so on. In short, this section tells new employees what the company expects from them.

- **Worker Benefits**

  Most companies offer *benefits* to their full-time workers. These include paid time off for vacations, holidays, and illnesses. Other benefits, such as health insurance, are explained in full detail. Some companies offer to pay part or all of school tuition if employees are taking work-related classes. By reading this section, new employees learn what they can expect from the company.

Use the above information to complete the sentences.

1. An employee handbook says that a new employee will have his or her first *work review* in 60 days. This information appears in the section entitled

   a. Introduction to the Company.

   b. Company Policies and Procedures.

   c. Worker Benefits.

2. Rules about how employees should dress, treat customers, and so forth are some of a company's

   a. benefits.   b. policies.   c. history.

3. Information laid out like this:

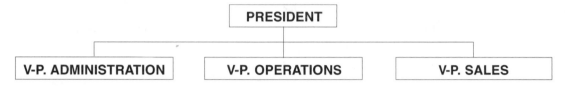

   is the top of a

   a. chart of organization   b. flow chart.   c. pie chart.

4. Until you have time to read the entire handbook, you can quickly locate information that is most important to you by

   a. asking the president for help.   b. speed reading.   c. checking the table of contents.

5. Paid time off because of illness or injury is often called

   a. downtime.   b. sick leave.   c. absenteeism.

6. The section in the employee handbook that explains what workers can expect from the company is called

   a. Worker Benefits.
   b. Policies and Procedures.
   c. Introduction to the Company.

7. Information laid out like the illustration on the right is the first part of a

   a. work order.
   b. job review.
   c. flow chart.

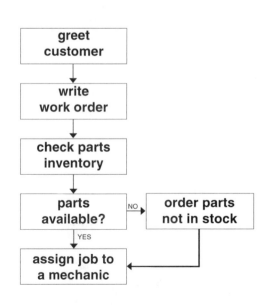

Starting a new job means having to quickly take in a lot of new information. Here are some tips to help you memorize more effectively.

MEMORY AIDS

1. **Be an active learner.** You are more likely to remember new information if you write it down or say it out loud than if you merely read it or hear it.

2. **Clarify any confusions.** If you don't understand a direction or instruction, ask someone to explain it further. It's very hard to remember what you don't understand.

3. **Associate new information with old.** When you're trying to learn something new, try to compare it with something similar that you are already familiar with.

4. **Use key words.** For example, to learn these memory aids, pick out a key word for each aid and learn just the key words. For items 1–4 the key words could be *active, clarify, associate,* and *key.*

5. **Visualize what you're trying to learn.** This can involve creating a mental image or drawing a chart (for example, listing people's names in order from the front of the office to the back).

6. **Group items into categories.** If you have to learn a long list of things, group similar items together. (It's easier to remember three lists of nine related items than one list of 27 unrelated items.)

7. **Focus on how many items are on the list.** If you can remember that there are six steps in processing an order, for example, it will help you to recall the six steps.

8. **Be selective.** Concentrate on general concepts (and a few examples of each) rather than trying to remember every detail. Pay particular attention to information your supervisor indicates is most important.

A

Think about the memorization techniques. Then circle a letter to show the best ending for each sentence.

1. Two ways of committing new information to memory are

   a. closing your eyes and breathing deeply.
   b. saying it aloud or writing it down.
   c. asking someone to remind you.

2. The best *key words* for tips 5 through 8 would be

   a. *create, list, number,* and *choose.*
   b. *visualize, group, number,* and *selective.*
   c. *learn, group, focus,* and *general.*

3. The information that you should memorize *first* is

    a. what your boss says   b. the company's   c. when you can
       is most important.   history.   go on vacation.

4. If you've just been hired to deliver mail to many different offices
in a big building, it might help you to make

    a. a floor map of   b. an alphabetical list   c. a list of employee
       the building.   of departments.   phone numbers.

5. It occurs to you that stocking the shelves in the office supplies
closet is a lot like putting groceries in your kitchen cupboards.
This memory technique is called

    a. selecting general concepts   b. associating new   c. brain-
       instead of details.   information with old.   washing.

B

**Use the clues to help you complete the crossword puzzle.
Answers are definitions of words you studied in Part A.**

ACROSS

1. to make clear or
understandable

4. alert, fully involved;
not passive

6. to focus only on
one thing

7. to put down on
paper

8. to say again

DOWN

1. groups of similar items

2. to imagine or mentally
picture something

3. describes words or ideas that are most important

5. to pay very close attention; to home in on

46 — PAYCHECK

Many young workers are unpleasantly surprised when they receive their first paycheck. Why? They didn't realize how much money would be taken out in deductions!

A

Read the glossary of "paycheck words."

GLOSSARY

deduction   amount of money subtracted from gross pay for a tax, a benefit, a service, or a membership

earnings statement   the check stub attached to your paycheck; it lists gross pay, deductions, and net pay

gross pay   amount of salary earned

net pay   amount of salary received after deductions have been taken out

tax   money paid into the national treasury or the state treasury

withheld   kept back

Unscramble the words to correctly complete the sentences.

1. Your **(SORGS YAP)** _____ is the amount of money you earned before deductions.

2. Federal tax is paid into the **(LONITANA)** _____ treasury.

3. When you cash your paycheck, the amount of money you receive is your **(ENT APY)** _____.

4. A **(TINOCUDED)** _____ is the amount of money **(HITHEWLD)** _____ to pay for something else.

5. Your check stub may show a deduction for a **(FEBTINE)** _____ such as health insurance.

B

Study the information on the earnings statements (paycheck stubs).
Then circle words to correctly complete the sentences.

Speed Co. Service Stations   EMPLOYEE: Cal Jackson

PAY PERIOD ENDING: 11/30   SOCIAL SECURITY NUMBER: 999-00-9999

GROSS PAY	FEDERAL TAX	STATE TAX	FICA	HEALTH INSURANCE	DISABILITY INSURANCE	UNION DUES	CREDIT UNION	UNITED FUND	NET PAY
$970.00	$108.00	$10.05	$72.85	$114.00					$665.10

The Chicken Hut   EMPLOYEE: Kim Wu

PAY PERIOD ENDING: 3/31   SOCIAL SECURITY NUMBER: 999-01-0009

GROSS PAY	FEDERAL TAX	STATE TAX	FICA	HEALTH INSURANCE	DISABILITY INSURANCE	UNION DUES	CREDIT UNION	UNITED FUND	NET PAY
$1,126.00	$132.00		$84.56	$114.00	$13.51		$10.50	$3.00	$768.43

Cityscape Computers, Inc.   EMPLOYEE: Rosa Cruz

PAY PERIOD ENDING: 6/30   SOCIAL SECURITY NUMBER: 999-12-3456

GROSS PAY	FEDERAL TAX	STATE TAX	FICA	HEALTH INSURANCE	DISABILITY INSURANCE	UNION DUES	CREDIT UNION	UNITED FUND	NET PAY
$1,280.00	$150.00	$21.25	$96.13			$36.50			$976.12

1. Net pay is always (less / more) than gross pay.

2. (Kim's / Rosa's) paycheck stub shows a deduction for union dues.

3. The deduction for Social Security must be indicated by the acronym
   (FICA / Credit Union) which stands for Federal Insurance Contribution Act.

4. Cal pays approximately (one-sixth / one-ninth) of his gross pay in
   federal tax.

5. (Kim / Rosa / Cal) is the only worker contributing to an association
   of charitable organizations.

6. The worker with the greatest total amount of deductions is (Cal / Kim).

7. Rosa's net pay is ($311.02 / $291.15) more than Cal's.

WORKING OVERTIME

A regular work week for most employees is 40 hours. That usually means working eight hours a day for five days. When a workplace is unusually busy, however, an employer may offer *overtime work*. Since overtime means extra pay, many workers are very happy to work the additional hours.

A

Circle a letter to correctly complete each sentence.

1. A restaurant waiter may be asked to work overtime if
   a. the waiter scheduled to work the next shift calls in sick.
   b. customers don't like the chef's "nightly special."
   c. the boss is feeling especially generous for some reason.

2. Clerks at a school supply store could probably get more overtime work
   a. in July rather than in March.
   b. in September rather than in June.
   c. if the store closed on holidays.

3. It makes sense for an employer to pay overtime rather than hire additional workers if
   a. the store will soon be doubling in size.
   b. everyone on the staff seems to be quite sickly.
   c. extra help is needed only in certain seasons.

Hourly employees get *time and a half* for working overtime. This means that for every hour (over 40) worked, employees get their regular hourly wage *plus* half that amount.

Suppose Harold usually earns $6 an hour, for example. When he works overtime, he would earn half that amount ($3) in addition to his regular wage for a total of $9 per hour.

B

Help the following employees compute their overtime pay. Write your answers on the lines.

1. Ike works 44 hours one week. His regular hourly wage is $7 per hour.

   Ike worked _____ hours of overtime. The extra pay he

   will receive for those hours is _____.

2. Patricia worked an extra 8-hour shift this week.
   Her regular wage is $6.50 per hour.

   Patricia's pay for her regular 40 hours of work is _____.

   Her pay for overtime work is _____.

   Her gross pay for the week is _____.

3. Delbert works part-time for $5.50 an hour. One week, instead
   of working his usual 30 hours, Delbert works an additional
   four-hour shift.

   Does Delbert get overtime for the extra four hours? _____

   How much was his gross pay for 34 hours? _____

4. Carly is a skilled keyboarder who earns $9.50 per hour.
   During a busy month, she worked Saturdays in addition
   to the regular workdays.

   How much extra money did Carly earn that month

   by working four Saturdays? _____

● ● ● ● ● ● ● ● ● ● ● ● ● ● ● **JUST FOR FUN** ● ● ● ● ●

Find the name of a *country* hidden in each sentence.
Hint: Parts of the name may be in one or more words.
The first one has been done for you.

1. I went to a lovely (spa in) the country last week. _____*Spain*_____

2. The child said, "I am Eric, a good little boy." _____

3. Can a dark window shade keep out the light? _____

4. In his father's den Mark does all of his homework. _____

5. The football hit Al yesterday on his nose. _____

6. His chin and jaw were also hurt. _____

7. Often glands do not function properly. _____

8. The dice landed on the floor when Al threw them. _____

GROUPS AND MEMBERS

Which is the group and which is the member? These analogies test your knowledge of general categories and specific examples.

EXAMPLES: group to member: *Team* is to *player* as *family* is to _sister_ .

member to group: *Wool* is to *fabric* as *lemon* is to _citrus_ .

jellyfish	sport	game	melon
sombrero	faith	tree	mineral
produce	candy	hat	carrot
animal	snake	golf	checkers

◆ Follow the directions. Try not to use a word more than once.

1. Study the words in the box. Choose one *group* and a *member* that belongs to that group. Write the words on the lines.

   group: _____   **member:** _____

2. Complete each analogy with a word from the box.

   a. *Plaid* is to *pattern* as *iron* is to _____.

   b. *Invertebrate* is to *worm* as *vertebrate* is to _____.

   c. *Grain* is to *wheat* as *vegetable* is to _____.

   d. *Doll* is to *toy* as *sycamore* is to _____.

   e. *Vice* is to *greed* as *virtue* is to _____.

   f. *Mustard* is to *condiment* as *fudge* is to _____.

3. Choose four words from the box to write an analogy relating a *group* to a *member*. Write your analogy on the line.

   _____

4. Choose four words from the box to write an analogy relating a *member* to a *group*. Write your analogy on the line.

   _____

A On the line after each sentence, write complete words for each abbreviation.

1. Gina hopes to become a secretary. She answers a classified ad for

   a **gen. off. asst.** _____

2. Tad wants to work 40 hours a week this summer. He answers

   an ad for a **F/T temp.** worker. _____

3. Michelle has never held a job. The job ad that interests her

   says **no exp. nec.** _____

4. Gerald goes to school during the day. He wants a job

   working **P/T eves.** _____

B Read the sentences. Then unscramble the words and write the correct words on the lines.

1. A company's policies and procedures are explained in its

   employee **(HOKADNOB)** _____.

2. **(CISK VEALE)** _____ is one benefit of a full-time job.

3. An **(CAVIET)** _____ learner can memorize more

   easily than a passive learner can.

C Use words from the box to complete the analogies. *Hint:* You will *not* use all the words.

fight	book	army	banana	apples
several	singer	sailor	roses	encyclopedia

GROUP TO MEMBER:

1. *Cluster* is to *grape* as *bunch* is to _____.

2. *Collection* is to *stamp* as *chorus* is to _____.

MEMBER TO GROUP:

3. *Knight* is to *chessmen* as *volume* is to _____.

4. *Colonist* is to *colony* as *soldier* is to _____.

A Choose a word from the box to complete each pair of *synonyms* or *antonyms*. Write the words on the lines. *Hint:* You will *not* use all the words.

distribute	bake	caution	comply	portions
pesticide	blend	irritate	home	natural
voluntary	tools	refill	dried	repeat

———————————————— **SYNONYMS** ————————————————

1. servings—_____

2. poison—_____

3. obey— _____

4. utensils— _____

5. warning— _____

6. residence— _____

———————————————— **ANTONYMS** ————————————————

1. soothe—_____

2. separate—_____

3. gather—_____

4. synthetic— _____

5. refrigerate— _____

6. marinated— _____

B Circle the hidden words in the puzzle. The words may go up, down, across, backward, or diagonally. Check off each word as you find it.

____ INGREDIENTS

____ VOLATILE

____ BEREAVEMENT

____ WARNING

____ UTENSIL

____ GROOMING

____ COLORFAST

____ FABRIC

____ LIMITED

____ CATEGORY

____ MINCE

____ AMOUNT

```
F O V U T E N S I L D H B
W A L O C L G D S C E S E
S R E N L A A Y T U T B R
E R I E M A R S N N I Y E
I M E O E O T D E S M X A
L N U T G L V I N D I P V
H N O E H A D C L N L Q E
T Y T B O E D Y I E H U M
P A W A R N I N G R E A E
C R E G S E N E Y M B S N
L G N I M O O R G O G A T
M I C O L O R F A S T F F
```

C First, cross out the word that *doesn't* fit in each category. Then classify the words in the box by *adding* the appropriate word to each category. Write the words on the lines. *Hint:* You will *not* use all the words in the box.

nominee	temperature	deadline	solemn
setting	classify	travel	scale

1. **MAP WORDS**

    equator   longitude   republic   _____

2. **CALENDAR WORDS**

    appointment   dictionary   priority   _____

3. **LITERATURE WORDS**

    calculate   dialogue   narrator   _____

4. **ELECTION WORDS**

    vote   majority   timeline   _____

D Write **T** or **F** to show whether each statement is ***true*** or ***false***.

1. _____ The letters in the word **SERGED** are not *in sequence*.

2. _____ World War II began with the German occupation of Poland.

3. _____ *Fence is to enclose as ruler is to measure* is an analogy relating *synonyms*.

4. _____ A *syllogism* is composed of one premise and two conclusions.

5. _____ Under the Articles of Confederation, only Congress could print money.

6. _____ Edgar Allan Poe was the hero of C. Auguste Dupin's detective stories.

E Circle words to correctly complete the sentences.

1. (Inference / Infancy) is the skill of using reasoning to arrive at a sensible conclusion.

2. The top of a city map shows streets in the (eastern / northern) part of the city.

3. Airport monitors give you current information about (ticketing and fares / arrivals and departures).

4. On a city map, the (index / scale) uses letter-number pairs to help you locate streets.

5. Many (national / neighborhood) community centers offer classes to residents of the area.

6. You could look at a (route map / floor plan) to find out which bus goes downtown.

F Unscramble the words to correctly complete the sentences. Write the words on the lines.

1. Grace and Shandra will shop at the **(ALLM)** _____ for school clothes.

2. Paul **(NACSS)** _____ the assigned chapter to get a general idea of what it's about.

3. To get to the library, Katie must **(FRETSNAR)** _____ from one bus route to another.

4. Before he could practice driving, Brad had to get an instruction, or learning **(TRIMEP)** _____.

5. *Engine* is to *car* as *photo* is to driver's **(CLEENIS)** _____.

6. Week is to Thursday as mall is to **(ROTES)** _____.

G Circle a letter to show the correct answer to each question.

1. Which of the following words begins with a *prefix* and ends with a *suffix*?

   a. understand   b. advertisement   c. interactive

2. What might be the *effect* of an excellent job review?

   a. a promotion   b. termination   c. tardiness

3. What word would correctly complete the analogy, *staff is to receptionist as workplace is to _____*?

   a. location   b. office   c. policies

4. A CD priced at $14.99 is how much more expensive than another priced at $12.49?

   a. $2.50   b. $3.50   c. $1.50

5. The abbreviation *cln. driv. rec.* stands for which words below?

   a. cleaning deposit required   b. Calvin's Driving School   c. clean driving record

H *What can you avoid if you purchase with cash instead of credit?* Use the clues to complete the puzzle. The answer will read from the top to bottom.

1. charge for delivery of a catalog order

2. information booklet for new employees

3. You must write the _____ number on a catalog order form.

4. Is debt the cause or the _____ of not paying off a credit card balance?

5. A _____ is a group of letters such as *re, un,* or *sub.*

6. A _____ date is when a payment must be made.

7. A _____ is a group of letters such as *ist, ment,* or *ion.*

8. Apartments for _____ are listed in the classified ads.

1. __ __ | __ __ __ __ __ __
2. __ __ | __ __ __ __ __ __
3. __ | __ __ __
4. __ | __ __ __ __ __
5. __ | __ __ __ __ __
6. __ __ | __
7. __ | __ __ __ __ __
8. __ __ __ | __

READING COMPREHENSION GLOSSARY OF TERMS

❶ Abbreviation

An abbreviation is a shortened form of a word or phrase.

v. for *verb*
Pres. for *President*
etc. for *etcetera*

Most abbreviations end with a period, but some do not.

ABC for *American Broadcasting Company*
IL for *Illinois*   *CA* for *California*

❷ Analogy

An analogy is a statement of relationship between two things. Many standardized tests require you to complete analogies. There are many different kinds of analogies including the following:

opposites: *Hot* is to *cold* as *in* is to *out.*
synonyms: *Tiny* is to *small* as *huge* is to *big.*
action/object: *Hammer* is to *pound* as *pen* is to *write.*
characteristics: *Sweet* is to *sugar* as *wet* is to *rain.*

❸ Antonym

Antonyms are words that mean the opposite or nearly the opposite of one another.

plain/fancy
always/never
shout/whisper

❹ Boldfaced

Boldfaced type is heavier and darker than regular type. It is used for emphasis.

*Write **only** on lines marked by arrows.*

❺ Category

A category is a division of a main subject or group; a class.

The two *categories* of Biology are Zoology and Botany.

❻ Cause and Effect

A cause is a person or thing that brings about some action or result (the effect of the cause). Identifying causes and effects is an important reading skill.

cause: *icy streets*
effect: *traffic accidents*

❼ Chronological

Chronological order lists things in the order in which they happened; the same as time order.

first, second, third
Civil War, World War I, World War II

❽ Connotation

A word's connotation is the idea or feeling it suggests in addition to its actual meaning.

Calling a person a *snake* connotes sneakiness and meanness.

❾ Contrast

To contrast two or more things is to compare them in ways that show differences.

The contrast between air travel and train travel reveals significant differences in speed and comfort.

❿ Denotation

A word's denotation is its exact literal definition, as it would appear in a dictionary.

A snake is a crawling reptile.

⓫ Figurative Language

Figurative language is colorful, imaginative wording intended to create a sharp picture in the mind of the reader. The meaning of the words in a figurative expression are different from their literal meanings.

screaming headlines
babbling brook
"Take a hike!"

⑫ Graph

A graph is a pictorial representation of factual information. Charts and diagrams are graphs.

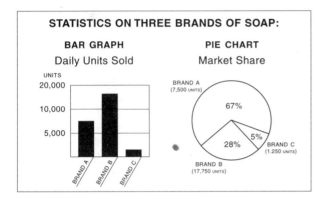

⑬ Inference

You make an inference when you arrive at a conclusion or form an opinion by reasoning. Inference is a major reading skill.

*Harry's remark **implied** that I stole the necklace. Since I didn't do it, I **inferred** that Harry himself might be the thief.*

⑭ Italic

An italic typeface, which slants upward and to the right, is used for such things as book titles, foreign words, and to call attention to certain words.

Uncle Tom's Cabin was written by Harriet Beecher Stowe.

⑮ Key

A key is something that explains something else, such as a list of answers to problems or a set of symbols for pronouncing words. A key on a map explains symbols or abbreviations.

⑯ Narrator

The narrator is the character who tells the story in his or her own words.

Ishmael is the *narrator* of *Moby Dick*.

⑰ Plot

A story's plot is the chain of events that leads to its outcome.

The suspenseful murder mystery had an exciting *plot*.

⑱ Prefix

A prefix is a group of letters added to the beginning of a word to change its meaning.

*un*earned   *re*stated
*non*violent   *in*flexible

⑲ Premise

A premise is a statement or belief that is taken for granted and used as the basis for an argument or conclusion.

The candidate's expected victory is based on the *premise* that her party has more registered voters.

⑳ Scan

To scan a written work is to look it over quickly before reading it thoroughly.

Matt *scanned* the chapter to get the general idea.

㉑ Sequence

Sequence is the order in which things follow one another.

January, February, March are months listed in *sequence*.

㉒ Setting

The setting of a story is the time and place in which the events happen.

Dr. Jekyll and Mr. Hyde is *set* in 19th century London.

㉓ Suffix

A suffix is a group of letters added to the end of a word to change its meaning.

sad*ness*   lone*ly*
honor*able*   moment*ary*

㉔ Syllogism

A syllogism is a form of reasoning in which two statements (premises) are made and a logical conclusion is drawn from them.

Children play with toys.
Kites are toys.
Children play with kites.

All citrus are fruits.
Lemons are citrus.
Lemons are fruits.

㉕ Synonym

Synonyms are words that have the same or nearly the same meaning.

happy/joyful
foliage/greenery
therefore/thus

㉖ Terminology

Terminology is the set of special words and phrases used in a certain work, study, sport, etc.

Doctors and nurses use medical terminology.

㉗ Word Analysis

Figuring out a word's meaning by looking at its parts is called word analysis. Many words have three parts: a base word or root, a prefix, and a suffix.

refundable
re (prefix: to do again or go back)
fund (base word)
able (suffix: capable of being)